Effective Financial Tools
for
SCIENTIFIC
MANAGERS

JAMES J. FARLEY

LEWIS PUBLISHERS

Boca Raton   Ann Arbor   London   Tokyo

Library of Congress Cataloging-in-Publication Data

Farley, James J.
    Effective financial tools for scientific managers / James J. Farley
       p.   cm.
    Includes bibliographical references and index.
    ISBN 0-87371-878-X
    1. Business enterprises—Finance.   I. Title.
HG4026.F37   1993
658.15—dc20
                                       93-11413
                                           CIP

© 1994 by CRC Press, Inc.
Lewis Publishers is an imprint of CRC Press

No claim to original U.S. Government works
International Standard Book Number 0-87371-878-X
Library of Congress Card Number 93-11413
Printed in the United States of America 1 2 3 4 5 6 7 8 9 0
Printed on acid-free paper

Preface

This book is written primarily for the aspiring technical manager on the way up the ladder. This technical manager may be brilliant in chemistry, physics, biology, or math; however, this person will—as he or she climbs up the ladder—find that business skills are needed; not just buzz words—they won't suffice. At this point in a career, for the good of the person and for the good of the company, business savvy is what is needed, not just business jargon.

Business today represents the merging of technological developments with market demand and, hence, a knowledge of technology and the business principles (and their actual applications) is what is needed in order to maximize profits. The phrase "maximize profits" will be mentioned much in this book, because that's what business is all about—to make a profit and to make the highest possible profit within the realm of time, economics, and ethics.

In the preparation of this text, I have tried to keep in strict accordance with this title and describe those business principles and applications which are most important for the technical manager to understand. This is to say that this is not to be a compilation of textbooks on each of the individual subjects of marketing, economics, etc. If the reader wants to buy a textbook on any one of the individual chapter headings or topics, there are a sufficient number of good ones available. This is, rather, intended to be what I believe could be *the first book of its kind* that touches on "just enough" of each of the topics to give the reader an understanding of what each one is. In Parts One and Two the business and the technical functions are described with their individual elements or topics. Part Three shows the integration of these elements to achieve the goal of selling the company's product or service, hopefully at a price greater than the cost to produce, which will result in a profit for the company. Once in a while a company sells a product at a price that is less than the cost to produce. This results in a loss. Rarely, this is done deliberately when another product line will directly or indirectly profit. Sometimes, however, it is not realized until after the fact and rapid adjustments have to be made.

This book is meant to be a *practical* guide and is based on my true-to-life experiences and observations.

During the course of this book, the product or service will be referred to as a product to avoid an overuse of verbiage. If your company produces a service, then consider the service a product.

A review of the content of this book will show that it is not just a book for the technical manager who wants to learn business. It is also intended to be a very good reference for the business person—sales, marketing, manufacturing, etc.—who is on the move upward and must learn something about the technological function. In fact, I believe that if the business persons read this book and the technical persons read this book they then can attend meetings that will be much shorter in duration and have greater communication, and they can feel much better upon leaving the meeting.

The reader can use this book as a reference in communicating and negotiating with other persons in other areas within the company. This text will enable the reader to know more about the overall integrated functions of a company, be more productive to the company, and progress up the ladder in personal achievement and reward.

James J. Farley

Dedication

To my sons and daughters
Maryanne, Jim, Maureen, Theresa, and John
from whom I have learned much and will continue to do so

Acknowledgments

There are several persons whose assistance should be recognized. They helped me directly or over the phone or through correspondence and by sending me encouraging notes in the process of writing this book. They are Harvey Mackay, President of Mackay Envelope Company, Minneapolis, Minnesota, and author of *Swim with the Sharks Without Being Eaten Alive, Beware the Naked Man Who Offers You His Shirt,* and *Shark Resistance;* Paul Hawken, former Principal of Smith and Hawken Company, Mill Valley, California and author of *Growing a Business;* and Alan R. Tripp, author of *Millions from the Mind.*

Acknowledgment is also given to Paul Noakes of Motorola and to James T. Egan, Corporate Consultant, for their courtesy and contributions.

Special thanks to Marilyn Jolles for constructive suggestions, several good ideas, and proofreading.

Thanks to Steve Koniers for many of the illustrations.

Thank you all for your encouragement and information.

About the Author

Jim Farley has 25 years of experience in the pharmaceutical and pharmaceutical packaging industries. He has managed a quality control laboratory and a technical service department, and has formed and directed a research and development laboratory in industry.

He has prepared and delivered training seminars for several professional training organizations. Currently Jim is adjunct instructor at Penn State University, Philadelphia area campus where he instructs various management subjects. He also teaches Physical Chemistry at Rosemont College and Finance and Marketing at Cabrini College. Having an MS in physical chemistry and an MBA in marketing and finance helps Jim to understand and teach the symbiosis of the technical and business areas.

Jim is employed as Director of the Science Branch at the Philadelphia District of the Food and Drug Administration.

The combination of industry, academic, and federal government experience provides a unique background and viewpoint that Jim utilizes in his everyday business and technical activities.

Contents

Part 2
The Elements of the
Technical Area

PART 1

THE ELEMENTS

CHAPTER **1**

Business: An Overview

A business is formed, and exists, so that its owners can produce and sell something with the proceeds being equal to more than what it costs to produce and sell it. This leads to what is called a profit.

Some firms don't do this. They sell at a figure that is less than what it costs them to produce and deliver the item. With regard to these firms, some do it deliberately and call it a "loss leader," which is a product that is sold at a loss on the premise that when the customers purchase it they will see other items sold by the same firm and buy them with a resulting net profit due the firm. Some, however, sell at a loss and don't realize it until it's too late.

INTERRELATIONSHIPS OF THE VARIOUS BUSINESS AREAS

A business can be pictured as a mobile where the central part of the mobile is attached to the ceiling or its balance plane, then various areas are balanced within that mobile, as illustrated in Figure 1-1. The mobiles that are for sale in stores resemble items that are suspended from the ceiling like a ship with small ships hanging from it at different lengths of line. When one of these is hit or displaced the entire mobile moves in an attempt to establish equilibrium. If there were a major change in one of those suspended items, say for instance, a weight was to be added to one, then the entire mobile would shift position in order to attain equilibrium. A

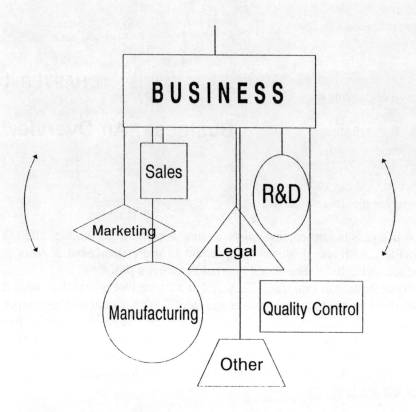

Figure 1-1.

business is just like that. If a major change is made in any one of the areas, the other areas must adapt in order to attain equilibrium.

For example, if research and development designs a new product, then marketing and sales must make suitable changes in their activities, quality control procedures must be designed for the new product, and the manufacturing facility must be geared up to produce the item. This situation occurs in many things. For example, on a personal basis, an individual person is comprised of various aspects such as career, social, religious, etc. When there is a major displacement in any one of these, the other areas will shift in order to attain equilibrium. An example of this is when a person becomes unemployed. Other activities will adjust accordingly.

Religiously, the person may pray more or less. Socially, the person may be more restrained, or may venture out more in an effort to ease the burden of this unemployment situation.

With regard to a particular department in a business, if a major item of equipment is purchased, persons must be trained to operate that equipment and/or more persons must be brought on staff. Again, there is a shifting of the various components, i.e., people, within the department in order to get back to the equilibrium status.

On a global basis, the world as we know it is like this. If there is a major change, say a shortage of oil from a particular country, then the economies of many other countries must adapt in some fashion in order to compensate for this, and, in some manner, try to get back to their equilibrium states.

A manager in business must manage his own area, but at the same time must realize the relations to other areas. There is much interfacing among the various areas of research and development, manufacturing, marketing, sales, quality control and others, as has already been mentioned. The higher up the manager is, the more important this is, because the ramifications are greater.

An interesting aspect of this situation is that when a large change occurs in one area, the other areas will relate to that change in such a way as to attain an equilibrium situation; however, while this is always tried, it is never reached. The reason for this is because as that state is nearly reached, the business must shift to higher goals, again disrupting the equilibrium. This is the way it should be. This is the way people are. When they achieve a particular goal, say a promotion at work, then they work to perform at that, but at the same time immediately set the next higher goal which is the next promotion sometime in the future. Then, they work toward that higher goal.

The way business does this is that as management sees that a goal is being achieved, for example, a particular market share is reached and a particular sales volume is reached (or nearly reached), then new products or new applications of existing products are designed to increase sales beyond that point. Maybe money has to be borrowed in order to facilitate a plant expansion, and so on. This is to say that the equilibrium, when it is nearly attained, is then shifted forward. Therefore, it is never really reached. If it were to be reached, then the firm would not be looking forward enough. So this apparent paradox is, in reality, what is desired in business.

FORMS OF BUSINESS ORGANIZATION

In business, there are three primary forms of business organization. They are the sole proprietorship, the partnership, and the corporation. It is important to know the differences among these three forms and the advantages and disadvantages of each. There are some businesses that start out as partnerships and then transform into corporations at such a time as is determined to be most beneficial for the firm. There are some that start out as corporations. There are some that are sole proprietorships and remain as such. Now, the three different types will be presented.

Sole Proprietorship

The sole proprietorship is a business owned by one individual person. It is easy to set up. In effect, a person simply starts doing business. It is in reality, a little more complicated than that. Many cities and states require licenses in order for an individual to do business. (Of course, a business person would want to get set up with various insurance policies such as disability insurance, etc. While this is an important aspect, it is not a requirement of doing business. It would not be very smart to do business without this insurance, but what is being discussed here are the requirements for doing business.)

The sole proprietorship has some significant advantages. One of these is that it is easy and relatively inexpensive to form. Also, no formal charter for operations is required, and it is usually subjected to fewer government regulation than larger businesses such as corporations. The business does not pay corporate income taxes, which are usually a higher rate than individual taxes. However, there is an important point to consider here. With a corporation, any earnings that are reinvested in the business result in a tax deduction. In a sole proprietorship, the earnings of the firm are subject to personal income taxes. The individual proprietor will want to make some decisions regarding how much to reinvest in the business as a sole proprietorship.

There are some limitations to the proprietorship. Since it is relatively small and is owned by a single individual it is difficult for the proprietorship to obtain large amounts of capital for expansion or whatever. It is, at the same time, a little bit unusual for a proprietorship to undergo a major expansion such as doubling or tripling in size. If this is going to be the case, one might consider reestablishing into an alternative form of business like a corporation. Additionally, the proprietor has *unlimited personal liability* for the business that can lose assets beyond those owned by the company. This is to say that the proprietor can lose a personal car, a house, a boat and more, if a significant debt is incurred or if the business is sued by someone. In real life, the nature of the business is associated with the probability of such a lawsuit occurring. In certain businesses, such as shoe manufacturing and selling, the possibility is very remote. However, in other businesses, such as food establishments where people can either complain about being poisoned by the food or slip on a banana peel and incur serious injury, the probability increases.

Another aspect is that the life of the proprietorship is limited to the life of the individual who started it. This means that when the owner dies, the business ceases to exist. The assets are divided up among the heirs, the debtors, and the government. In many cases, an heir or some other individual will immediately restart the business, and, as far as the public knows, it is that same business continuing on. In reality, and legally, the business dissolved and a new proprietorship was formed.

Many businesses are started as proprietorships and then are changed into corporations when their growth causes the disadvantages of the proprietorship to outweigh the advantages. Many firms convert over to the corporate structure even though there is a higher tax rate, because there are significant tax deductions and other benefits associated with this.

Partnership

A partnership is similar to a proprietorship except that it is a business owned by two or more persons. Specifically, it is an unincorporated business owned by two or more persons. The advantages and disadvantages are the same as with the sole proprietorship. It is easy to form, such as when two or more persons get together and decide to form the partnership, and it does not pay corporate income taxes; the individual partners are taxed on the income from the business, distributed proportionately between them as they previously agreed, as personal income. The partnership has similar disadvantages to the proprietorship, the first being that of unlimited liability. Note here that if there are two partners and there is a major problem with the business and one partner disappears for any reason, such as "taking off for a foreign country, whereabouts unknown," the courts will find the remaining partner and that partner will be responsible for all of the debt of the partnership. Essentially, what the courts do is get whomever they can find and make them pay. So it is important to note that if you are in a partnership, keep close track of the whereabouts of your partners.

Also, keep close track of what your partners are doing. If a partner starts purchasing luxurious vacations, boats and other frivolous things in the name of the business, you are responsible for payment of those.

The organization also has limited life. If a partner dies, the partnership ceases to exist. Again, as with a sole proprietorship, a new business can immediately be formed—that is, a new partnership with the remaining partners, or any restructuring they care to have, and the general public need not even be aware of this. As far as the general public is concerned the business lived on. In reality, from the legal sense, the partnership ceased and a new one began.

There is a difficulty in transferring ownership. This is a similar difficulty to getting people to agree on things. The more people there are, the more difficult it is to get them to agree on anything.

The tax treatment is very similar to that of a proprietorship. An important point to remember is that in a partnership consisting of two persons the profits are not necessarily divided 50/50 and in a partnership involving three persons, the profits are not necessarily divided 33%, 33%, 33%. They are divided in a manner that is agreed upon at the beginning of the partnership, usually in proportion to the amount of money put in by each individual, but not necessarily that way. Other things may be considered such as number of hours invested each week in the business by an individual. One may work 60 hours a week and another may work 30 hours a week and this would come into play in determining the returns given to each individual.

Corporation

A corporation is a legal entity created by a state. It is an entity in its own right. It is separate and distinct from its owners and managers, having unlimited life. It is easy to transfer ownership and it has limited liability.

The aspect of being separate and distinct from its owners and managers actually gives the corporation major advantages. It has *unlimited life*. Its life will continue after the original owners are deceased or have left the organization for whatever reason. It is easy to transfer ownership because the ownership is divided into shares of stock which is transferred significantly more easily than the ownership interests of a partnership or a proprietorship. It also has limited liability. Here's an example of this. If you purchase $5,000 worth of stock of a corporation and then that corporation had financial problems and ended up owing huge amounts of money, the maximum amount you can lose is your initial $5,000 investment. The corporation, itself, as an entity, is responsible for the entire debt. There are times when the corporation itself cannot pay its debts and then it goes bankrupt. In a proprietorship, you would be responsible for all the debts incurred and would have to use up to the limit of your personal assets to pay for this. In a partnership you would be held liable for the entire debt if your partners could not pay their parts. So you see, as a firm gets larger, this concept of limited liability alone is a worthwhile reason to consider incorporating.

There is a concept of double taxation that is associated with corporate earnings. (In society today, we often pay tax on income over and over, such as using your already taxed income to purchase theater tickets which have an amusement tax put on them.) The actual concept of double taxation involves the earnings of the corporation being taxed first before dividends are distributed, and then, after dividends are distributed to the shareholders they are taxed as income to the shareholders. This is what the concept of double taxation refers to when speaking of a corporation.

The comparisons of the three forms of business organization are shown in Figure 1-2.

Some Variations

There are some variations to the above three and they are discussed now. The first is with regard to partnerships. There is an organization that can be called a Limited Partnership. This consists of one or more general partners and several limited partners. The general partner or partners usually make the decisions for the partnership and in all the other respects have more to gain and more to lose. The limited partners put up money. They are limited in the amount they can lose. They won't lose any more than what they put up. They are also limited in the amount that they can gain, since a general partner is not going to make a fantastic return on investment available to a limited partner. They are also limited in what they can say about the activities of the organization—they usually have nothing to say about the direction or the decisions. Usually, the general partner has the greater responsibilities, more to gain, and makes all the decisions. The facts are presented to the individuals who will decide whether or not to be a limited partner, and then, if they decide positively, they become limited partners which is in effect putting up money with the hopes of a reasonably good return if the partnership is successful.

Relative comparison of three forms of business

	Sole Proprietorship	Partnership	Corporation
Formation	Easy	Easy	Some Effort
Raise Significant Capital	Difficult	Difficult	Easy
Liability	Unlimited	Unlimited	Limited
Life	As the Proprietor's	As the Partners'	Continuous
Taxes	As Personal Income	As Personal Income	Higher Rates as a Corporation

Figure 1-2.

If a person had much knowledge about a particular field or project and had some money available, but not sufficient funds, that individual would possibly consider a limited partnership. This would, in effect, be the recruiting of partners who would put up the money and let the general partner continue to run the organization. Of course, as with all good business deals, all the details would be put in writing at the time of formation.

The other variation to the forms described above is a Subchapter S Corporation. This is named this way because it is authorized under Subchapter S of the Internal Revenue Service (IRS) Code. With this formation, a smaller business can be formed as a corporation to limit the liability of the organization and to be able to obtain shareholders. It cannot have more than 35 shareholders—that is not permitted by the IRS. The primary advantage to this is that the income is taxed as personal income, which for a smaller business will usually result in a lower rate than the corporate tax rate. Therefore, the Subchapter S corporation form of business enjoys the limited liability of a corporation and has the advantage of a usually lower tax rate.

The regular corporate structure that was described previously, and that is usually considered when talking of corporations, by the way, is a Subchapter C Corporation.

GOALS OF THE BUSINESS

Most finance textbooks and other business textbooks will define the goal of a corporation as "to maximize shareholder wealth." This means to maximize the value of the common stock which means that the stockholders will be holding stock in the corporation that is worth as much as it can be worth.

Management of a corporation will have, in addition to the motivation of running a successful business, motivation in that management usually owns significant amounts of stock. In fact, stock bonuses are a common incentive when recruiting and holding top management personnel.

The question can always be raised whether or not the stock price was maximized. For example, if at a point in time a company's stock sold at $18.00 per share and then a year later it was selling at $25.00 per share and management was very pleased with this, any stockholder could always inquire whether with more effort or productivity the stock could not have been $26 or $28 or $30 or whatever. So you see, what really is the maximum is a question that is difficult to answer. Usually, reasonable gains are satisfactory.

In a partnership or a proprietorship, while there is usually no such thing as stock, the shareholder wealth is the equivalent of "owners' equity." Since there is usually no stock, there's no stock to maximize. Actually, for any kind of business, whether it is called owners' equity or shareholder wealth, the net profit is the "bottom line." In any business the owners or managers always try to maximize the profit or, in plain words, to make as much profit as they can.

In a very simplistic form, the accounting equation defines the situation: Assets - Liabilities = Equity. This is a rather obvious equation but it tells the story, and that story is told the same way whether it's a corner delicatessen or whether it's Exxon Corporation. The assets minus the liabilities equal the equity in a company, or, the net worth of that company.

PHILOSOPHIES OF A COMPANY

A company has a philosophy just like individuals have philosophies or styles. A company is set up as illustrated in Figure 1-3. For a corporation, the shareholders elect the board of directors. The board of directors (more will be said about this board of directors shortly) hires the Chief Executive Officer (CEO). The CEO reports to the board of directors. In turn, the

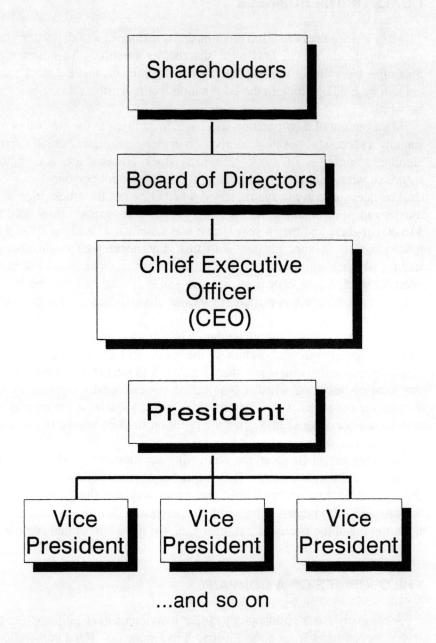

Figure 1-3.

president reports to the CEO, and the various vice presidents report to the president.

In a smaller corporation, one person may be the president and the CEO combined. Additionally, there may be no vice presidents. This all depends on the size of the corporation.

In a partnership, sometimes two or more partners act as president, CEO, etc., but the more common case is that one will function as president and CEO and another will function as vice president, treasurer, and secretary.

In a sole proprietorship, that person is everything. It's that simple. That person may not be called president or CEO but is in effect everything. On the other hand, that person doesn't have to report to any other person so all the decisions are made by one individual. Therefore, that individual is in effect the board of directors, the CEO, the president and all the other fancy titles rolled into one.

A company's "philosophy" means that the CEO will exhibit certain characteristics such as risk taking or risk avoidance, greater or lesser emphasis on research and development orientation, very secretive, or very open, etc. The president and the vice presidents will reflect philosophies similar to that of the CEO. Since the vice presidents report to the president, who in turn reports to the CEO, they will exhibit similar philosophies. If they do not, they won't last long with the company. Theoretically, the CEO is reflecting the philosophy of the company. Let's give an example. If the chief executive officer, as a reflection of the board of directors and therefore the company, is prone to avoid risks (as many are), then, this property will be exhibited by the various members of top management. If you are a department head and you are a risk taker, you are philosophically different than the company as reflected in the top management. Sooner or later you or the top management will have to go. Sometimes they do; more often than not it will be you. You may be an exceptionally talented individual, but if you have a philosophy or a style that is significantly different from that of the company, as exhibited by the top management, you will not only feel more comfortable elsewhere, you will be able to move up the line elsewhere because you certainly will not move up the line in your present company. Top management will not move you up the line when you have a philosophy that is different from theirs.

This is not a matter of equal opportunity for all. It's common sense. Top management only wants other top managers like themselves with regard to the style of thinking. If you have a drastically different style, such as the contrast illustrated above, then you'll be at odds with top management. Why should they have you there? If one of you has to go, it will usually be you. Recognize this early and if you can't find some way to change the top management, then realize what your style is with regard to risk taking, with regard to open or secretive policy, etc., and find a company that has that same philosophy. That's where you will move up the line, and you will do it readily. Why? Because you exhibit the same philosophy as the company. Assuming you have the fundamental talents that you should have, now you are with a company that treats you as one of its own. It not only makes good sense—that's the way it is.

RELATIVES IN A BUSINESS

Some businesses have a staff of relatives and close friends. If this is a small business, say up to $10 or $20 million per year, and there are relatives in the business, such as father and sons and daughters, and you are not a relative, then you should get out even faster than when you have a different philosophy. If they really need you, you will be favored as long as they need you. Other than at that time, you must remember that "blood is thicker than water."

This is a fact. Many presidents have been heard to say something to the effect of, "That guy's a real foul-up, but he's my sister's kid. I have to leave him heading the division, even if he's running it into the ground."

Remember, you may be extremely talented, but the relatives see each other at family dinners and social events, etc. You are simply a person in their employ. Here again, recognize the situation and get out to where you're appreciated and can move on up the line as rapidly as you feel you should.

PLANNING

An important aspect of any business is planning. This will be mentioned many times throughout this book in different settings. Put quite simply, "If you don't know where you're going, how will you ever know if you got there?"

While there are various texts that will list different numbers of elements in a plan, sometimes 8, sometimes 10, sometimes more, there are really only 5. They are:

• Where do you want to go, or, what do you want to do?
• What does it take to get there, or what does it take to do it?

Where do you want to go?

What does it take to get there?

Make the decision

Implement (do it)

Monitor, Feedback

Figure 1-4. Farley's Five Steps in Planning.

- Make the decision.
- Do it! (sometimes called *implement*).
- Follow up. Get feedback. Also called *monitor.*

These are illustrated in Figure 1-4.

Let's give an example. If you want to take a ride in a boat, you have to determine where you want to go. Then once you determine where you want to go, you look on the charts and determine how far it is, and then you figure out how much fuel you'll need, how much food, and other things such as that. Then you make the decision to take the trip or not take the trip. In some respects this decision takes one millisecond, or the decision can take a long, long time depending on what you consider the decision making process, and how fast you are at making decisions. The next step is *do it!* Get in the boat and start the trip. Then, the last step is monitor. This means look at where you're going because the wind, the ocean currents, the tides, all can—even if you calculated carefully—have thrown you off course. Now, comes an important point. If you are going off course, before you make an immediate correction, look at where you're going. Maybe the port that you're heading for is better than the one you planned to go to. If you then determine that it is, reset your course toward that. This means you have to recalculate the food, the fuel, and all the other things and determine if you can still make it on this trip or if you have to return and get more supplies. On the other hand, if it is not as good as where you were heading, then make your correction and head toward the port of original destination, checking of course to make sure you still have enough supplies on board and can still complete the trip.

This analogy of a boat trip, perhaps a trip of only a few miles, serves well to illustrate the goals of a business. When you take the goals of a business, the many individual goals such as market share, number of new products, sales, profit and so on, all can be compared to this analogy. Again, we have from the small neighborhood delicatessen up to the Fortune 500 corporation, the same elements present in the planning process. And always remember that you want to know where you're going before you set out on a trip in the business world.

CHAPTER 2

Marketing

Marketing is a function that has many aspects. Some people use the terms sales and marketing interchangeably. Actually they are very different, although sales is one of the functions of marketing.

While sales is "only" one of the activities accomplished by the marketing function, it is, of course, a very important one. In fact, I'll go on record as saying that when you have a company that is starting to grow, and you want to hire one person to help your company grow, that person that is most important to your company is the salesperson. This is based on the premise that you already have your product. You need your product first. Then, you get the people who will get you the sales.

More will be said about sales in the next chapter; however, it was important to distinguish that there is a difference in the sales and marketing functions. We will now speak about:

- Marketing research
- Customers
- Differential advantage
- Consumer demographics
- Consumer decision process
- Cognitive dissonance
- Product life cycle

MARKETING RESEARCH

This involves finding out what your potential customers want, but there is much more to it. You also have to be aware of what's going on with the economy, and be knowledgeable about your competition. Your product is one item in this scenario. You have to answer such questions as: What is the current state of the economy? Is it such that people will purchase my product at this time? Where's my competition? Is my competition offering a better product in some way? Does the customer believe he needs the product I am offering? Can I make the customer believe he needs the product I am offering? Can I make the customer believe it to the extent that he will purchase the product? What must I do to make sure the customer purchases my product and not my competitor's?

Surveys play a large role in marketing research. However, you must realize that what people do is not always what they say they'll do. A typical case is in a shopping mall where a survey is taken and the typical question is "Would you buy the following product...?" Most people will answer that they will, and then they go on and buy a competitor's product when they see that the price may be a little bit less or maybe it may be a fancier package that caught their eye. Remember what people say they will do is not always what they really will do. In fact, in some cases, it is seldom what they will do. In fact, the more money that is involved in the transaction, the less likely it is that they will do what they say they will do.

Maybe you and I always do what we say we will do, but many of those people "out there" don't, and they are your customers.

Test marketing—which is actually putting your product in the market-place where you can see and monitor the customer's purchasing behavior—is preferred. Here, you see what the customers are actually doing. It will cost you a bit more money to run a market test than it will to run a survey, but your results will be more accurate and you can predict your market better.

CUSTOMERS

A customer purchases an item in the belief that that item is needed. The key term here is perceived need.

For example, if you manufacture VCRs and you have data to indicate that just about every household has a VCR, then how will you sell more of your product? You can make people believe that every household should have 2 VCRs. This is especially true for those for households that have 2 or more television sets. If you can convince people that there are sometimes 2 shows on at the same time that they may want to tape, then you can show them a "need" to have a second VCR. Once you do this and the customer believes that there is a need to have a second one, now you have to show why they should buy yours instead of someone else's.

Whether you think that households need 2 VCRs or not is incidental. It's what the customer thinks or what you can make the customer think that's important.

DIFFERENTIAL ADVANTAGE

The reason why people should buy your product instead of a competitor's—once they have made the decision to buy somebody's product—is going to be the result of your differential advantage. Why should they buy your product instead of your competitor's? What's better for them about your product than your competitor's? Do you have:

- Lower prices?
- Better guarantee?
- More durable product?
- Better customer service, perhaps an 800 number for the customer to call?

What is your differential advantage? This is specifically why people will buy your product in preference to your competitor's after they have made the decision to buy the product.

CONSUMER DEMOGRAPHICS

This is what you use to *target* your market. Two major categories of marketing are *mass marketing* and *target marketing*. If you are selling newspapers you can put them in newspaper vending boxes and put them on any street corner and probably sell them all. This is mass marketing. If, on the other hand, you are selling BMWs, an expensive car, you want to study a little more about where you're going to locate your dealership and how you are going to advertise. You are certainly not going to put your dealership in a poor part of town, and you are not going to advertise your automobiles in magazines that are read mostly by low income families. On the contrary, you will place your dealership in a more affluent section of town or a ritzy suburb, and you will advertise in the magazines that are read by people whose incomes enable them to purchase BMWs. You are then doing target marketing.

The way you do target marketing is by utilizing your consumer demographics. Here is a set of demographics that could apply to a typical BMW purchaser. These are not necessarily those used by the Bavarian Motor Works. They are used here as an illustration and are hopefully somewhere in line with what the actual ones are. Let's say:

- Age of consumer 30-55 years old
- Annual income of consumer $50,000 to $150,000
- Percentage self employed and percentage employed by a corporation
- Type of geographic area where their business is conducted
- Type of geographic area where they reside

Now there are many demographic studies that can be performed. Let's be careful not to be overwhelmed with data. Some of the data may be useless. For example, you may obtain—at a significant price—data on the height or range of heights of typical BMW owners, but is that really significant? You may obtain data on whether they are or are not college graduates. That may or may not be significant. The key point here is when you gather your sets of data to perform your demographic profile of your consumer you're investing time and money to obtain this profile. Just pause and think of what characteristics will be necessary to describe a profile of your typical customer (or consumer, here used interchangeably, although the customer is the person who purchases the product and the consumer is the person who uses the product. More about this later.)

Get what you need for your target marketing but don't spend extra time and money getting a lot of statistics you don't need.

CONSUMER DECISION PROCESS

It is distinctly to your advantage to know the steps in the consumer decision process. They are shown in Figure 2-1. The steps are:

- Stimulus
- Problem awareness
- Information search
- Evaluation of alternatives
- Purchase
- Postpurchase behavior

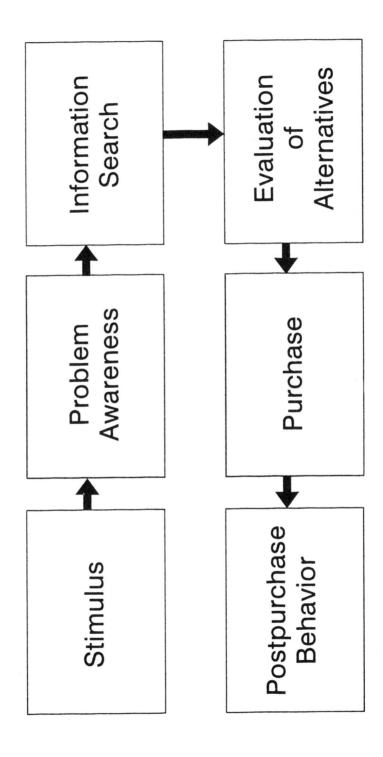

Figure 2-1. The Consumer's Decision Process.

Stimulus is whatever starts the process going. It can be the word of a friend, or something that you've seen in a newspaper ad or on a television commercial, or anything like that.

In *problem awareness,* the customer realizes that your product may solve a problem of his. That problem can be an unfulfilled desire. For example, a customer might see your advertisement for a suit and then realize that some of his are wearing out and purchase one of the suits that you are selling. That would solve his problem of having suits that are beginning to wear out.

The *information search* stage involves the customer gathering more information regarding the various products that are available to solve important problems, and finding the advantages and disadvantages of each. Putting it another way, the customer is searching for alternatives before locking in on your product.

Regarding the *evaluation of alternatives* stage, the customer is doing just that. There's not much more to say about this. In his own way, by whatever comparative mechanism the customer selects, he is evaluating the alternatives.

The next step is the *purchase.* After the customer has decided which is the best alternative, the decision to buy is made. (Some people consider actual decision as a separate step: here we're considering the decision to purchase and the purchase as one step.) Then the actual purchase is made. The purchase can be made over the phone, through the mail, dealing directly with you or your agent, or any other number of ways, but it certainly doesn't require a wealth of text to explain what the purchase is. That nebulous situation occurs when someone tells you they are going to buy but doesn't give you any money down on it. Is this a purchase or not? Well, that decision is up to you. It depends on your policies, how well you know the customer, what risks you're going to take, and various other factors such as those. So we won't get into an in-depth analysis of that. However, as a general guideline, you're the marketer—what makes you feel comfortable? If getting some money down in the form of cash or credit card, or whatever, makes you feel more comfortable than not getting it, then count that act as the purchase act.

In the *postpurchase behavior* stage, the customer, contrary to the good feeling that was obtained after making the decision to buy and making the actual purchase, now may experience feelings of regret. This is a psychological occurrence. The customer has had a good feeling of the purchase for several hours or even days, and now, the feelings involved with "did I make the right choice?" and "should I have spent that much money?" are coming into play. This is a strong feeling, that strength being determined by the magnitude of money involved and its value in the mind of the customer. A multimillionaire would not have strong regrets, if any, upon purchasing a $100,000 automobile whereas a person earning $20,000 or less would have serious second thoughts after making a purchase of a $10,000 compact car. This is an important feeling and must be considered. It will be in the next section. For now, remember the section on the Consumer Decision Making Process and know where you and your customer are at each point along the way.

COGNITIVE DISSONANCE

While postpurchase behavior may involve telling other people the good news about your product, it many times involves *cognitive dissonance*. As just mentioned, this is a strong psychological feeling and has to be handled accordingly. How do you do this? You take the active step and follow-up yourself; for example, if someone buys a washing machine from you, then, a few days after it's delivered, have something sent to them like a free box of detergent or a coupon for a free box of detergent. In the case of an automobile, you can call the customer and simply ask how they like it. Some people say that this causes the customer to raise questions. Well, if they don't like it they are going to call you anyway. If you believe in your product and you want the customer satisfied now, and you want that customer back again, and that customer to refer you to other customers, then it's certainly worth the time and effort.

You can probably think of many ways to follow-up the sale with your customer depending on your product and the natures of your customers.

PRODUCT LIFE CYCLE

The typical product life cycle is depicted in Figure 2-2. In the typical product life cycle as you see upon examining the graph—which is a plot of dollars versus time—in the introduction stage, the sales are slowly beginning. The next stage is the growth stage and here, as the name implies, the amount of sales are really being generated rapidly. In the maturity stage the sales continue up a bit but essentially "level out." This would not be bad if they continued along up there; however, the last stage is decline and that is when sales decrease and continue on downward.

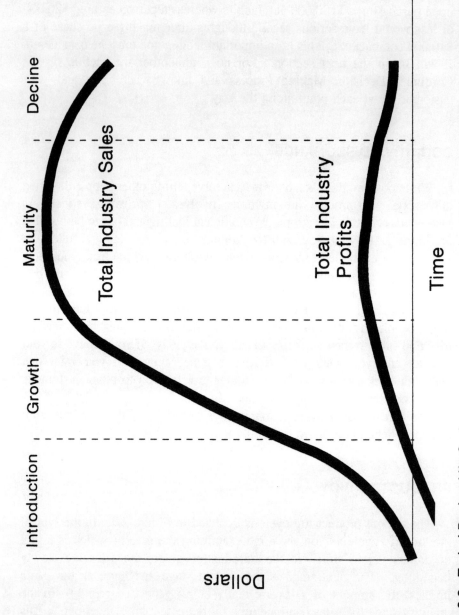

Figure 2-2. Typical Product Life Cycle.

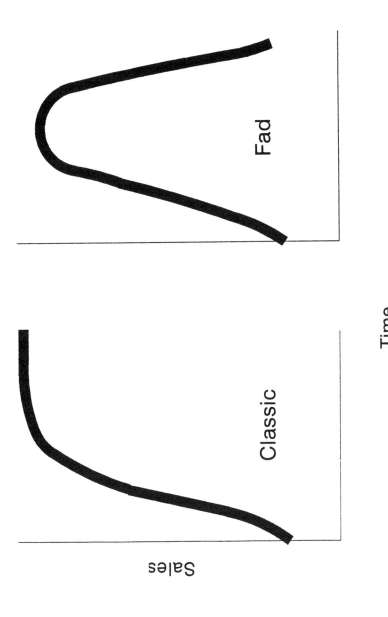

Figure 2-3.

The curve that is on the same graph, representing profit, shows a time lag between the sales and the time the actual profit was realized.

One of the key factors about the product life cycle is that when you bring something to the market you don't always know what the time frame involved in the life cycle will be. In fact, you seldom know.

At this time, no more manual typewriters are being manufactured, and therefore no new ones are being sold because no new ones are being made. The graph for a manual typewriter would indicate that this product has finished out its decline stage and actually is nonexistent (as a newly manufactured item). On the other hand you can draw separate graphs for electric typewriters, electronic typewriters, word processors, and computers with word processing programs.

If you want to draw a plot of the product "typewriters" and in your definition this would include *all* modern typewriters including the electronics and word processors, then, for this chart we are in the growth stage. You see, you can draw a chart representative of your product, as you define your product. We just showed the difference between plotting the graph for manual typewriters and plotting the graph for all kinds of typing machines.

There are other types of product life cycles. Observe Figure 2-3. The classic is something that has achieved a high level and continues at that high level. I certainly hope that "books" fall into this category since I am writing this one for you. Examination of the life cycle of a fad assures a rapid rise to the maximum and then a rapid decrease. This could be a particular fashion design that is only expected to have a short life cycle before a new one is introduced.

If you can know where you are in the life cycle of your product you can find ways to "stretch it out" at the maturity stage or design another product of yours that grows as this declines.

Remember, you can draw various life cycle curves, each for a different definition of a product. That is, if you use different degrees of specificity, you can end up with different life cycles. For example, the life cycle of an automobile has not hit the maturity stage yet. However, there are several kinds of automobiles that are no longer being produced—these have in the past reached their decline stage and the companies have actually gone out of the business.

Another way of looking at this is to remember that everything has a life cycle. Plants do, animals do, you and I do. In the case of ourselves, we hope the life cycle is a very long one. In the case of your product, you hope the life cycle is a very long one.

MARKETING YOUR TALENTS

One other thing that you want to seriously consider about the contents of this chapter is that you can use the principles of marketing in your career. You see, you actually market the various talents you have. We don't only market the product a company produces. We market ourselves and our opinions many, many times every day. In your career and in your movement up the line, you can use these marketing principles to market your talents to your employer.

Going back to the beginning of this chapter, ask yourself the question, "How can I market my talents to my employer and increase my employer's perceived need of me?" If you can do that, your career will be more successful than if you had not considered that.

CHAPTER 3

Sales

Sales is the direct contact with the customer. That in itself makes this very important since customers are the lifeblood of your business.

It was mentioned in the previous chapter that, after the product is designed, this is the first position to fill. Get a salesperson to generate the business for the company. Remember, sales is the area that brings the money in; the other areas do not bring money directly into the company. Quite the opposite—they spend it!

Many years ago when the Industrial Revolution came about, people ceased to routinely make their own things. Those who always made their own clothes now could go to the store and buy them. The same situation occurred with canning or preserving foods and with many other things that now could be purchased in a store. In fact, the demand was so great that people flocked to the stores to make the purchases. Keep that word "demand" in mind—it's the same word that's part of the supply/demand function that's a key part of business.

As the years went on, more products became available and the popularity of these products increased. In fact, for many, this shopping became fun. The sales function at this time consisted mainly of notifying the customers about what products you had and where those products could be purchased.

Now, as we arrive at current times, we find not only a tremendous number of products available, but competition that is at times intense. You need only to reflect for a few minutes to think of the large number of things that are available today that didn't exist 20 years ago. Microwave ovens for the home, VCR's and more. How does this change the sales activity? You have to tell the customer what you have, show them why they need it, and then, convince the customer to purchase yours. Didn't we say that about marketing in the previous chapter? Sure we did. Remember, sales is an integral part of marketing.

The subjects that we will cover in this chapter are:

- Who should be a salesperson? Where are they?
- The characteristics of a successful salesperson
- Who are your customers?
- Where are your customers?
- Industrial vs. General sales
- "Business to Business" vs. "Retail"
- Compensation Methods
- Segmentation: Territorial or Product
- The Sales Forecast
- Sales Managers

WHO SHOULD BE A SALESPERSON? WHERE ARE THEY?

The answers are everyone and everywhere. Certain persons carry the title and have the responsibility of selling the company's products. These are the ones we usually refer to as being "in sales." These are the ones that most chapters or books describe. We will concentrate on this aspect here, however, in business and in life we are all salespersons all the time.

When you are at a meeting and you want to convince others to see your point of view, you're selling. When you want to go to the ball game and another person wants to attend the opera and you try to persuade that person to go to the ball game, you're selling. When you try to tell the policeman that you didn't mean to be speeding and you shouldn't get a ticket, you're selling. When you explain to a potential employer that you should be hired, you're selling. Anytime you try to convince others to do as you want, you are selling your ideas, and you will be most effective if you use the same principles and techniques that the sales professionals use.

THE CHARACTERISTICS OF A SUCCESSFUL SALESPERSON

This has been a subject of speculation and wonder for many, many, years. It is obvious that, if you can categorize, or (remember marketing

terminology), define the demographic profile of a very successful salesperson, then you can search, find, and hire a super salesperson. Then your
company can make a lot of money.

There are various things that can be considered, such as education,
sociability, etc., but let's get to the things that really count. They are:

- High level of product knowledge. This is obvious of course, but the other
  side of the coin is that you don't have to be the engineer who designed
  the product but you do have to be able to describe the important points
  to your customer.
- A good planner. You must be able to plan your schedule and plan how
  you will handle each individual customer. You're dealing with people,
  and no two are identical. You may treat them equally but not necessarily
  identically.
- A good listener. Before you talk excessively about your product, listen
  to your prospect. You may have to ask a few questions initially like
  "How are the widgets that you're currently using performing?" Then
  listen. The statements that your prospect makes indicate satisfaction or
  areas of dissatisfaction. These areas of dissatisfaction indicate problems
  and if you and your product can solve these problems you have a new
  customer. Of course, if they are already buying from you and have a
  problem, you had better solve it fast!
- Have a good personality and be people oriented. This is readily apparent.
- Really believe that your customer is better situated for purchasing your
  product than for not buying it. If you really are sure in your own mind
  that you are helping the customer by selling him your product, this will
  come across in your presentation and you will optimize your probability
  of a sale.

WHO ARE YOUR CUSTOMERS?

We should begin by differentiating between purchasers and consumers.
Sometimes these terms are used interchangeably but they should not be.
Think of what the terms mean. The purchaser is the person who actually
purchases, or buys, your product. The consumer is the person who actually
consumes or uses, the product that they, or someone else bought for them.
Most things that you use you probably bought for yourself. However,
when someone bought a gift for you, that someone was the purchaser or
buyer, and you were the consumer. Of course, when you buy a gift for
someone else you are the buyer and that person is the consumer.
So...who's the customer—the purchaser or the consumer? Well, the first

thought could lead you to believe that the answer is the purchaser. In most cases, this will be correct. In some cases, it's the consumer even though someone-else made the purchase. Here's an example. Most, or at least a large number of men's ties are purchased by women. In some cases the lady got the idea, made the selection and then bought the tie. In some cases however, the gentleman hinted strongly that he wanted a tie for his birthday and also hinted strongly what style. (You say that if he hinted that strongly he's not a gentleman! That's a separate subject.)

The same situation occurs the other way around. With women's perfumes, many times the man is the purchaser and the lady is the consumer. By now you have the idea that the purchaser and the consumer may be two different persons. All this still leaves unanswered the question regarding who the customer is. Think about it for a minute! The customer that you want to convince is the person who is the decision maker or, who influences the other person significantly enough to direct the decision. That's the person who is your potential customer.

WHERE ARE YOUR CUSTOMERS?

In it's most simplistic form the answer is one of the following:

- They are already buying from you. Find a way to sell them more.
- They are buying from your competition. Find a way to get them away from the competition. Find an advantage of your product over the competition's. It may be in the physical product, the customer service, or better delivery.
- They are not buying from anyone. Find a way to get them interested in your product and to buy from you.

Once you determine where your customers are, i.e., in which of the locations just mentioned, then you direct your marketing efforts accordingly. Direct those efforts by targeting your market, according to its demographic profile, as described in the previous chapter.

Your easiest, or most dependable, or best, or whatever you want to call it, method, is to get repeat sales from existing customers or to get referrals from them.

The ones dealing with your competitor may not know about you (certainly your competitor's not going to tell them!), or, since they have a product source, are not actively searching for another. Maybe they need to know that you're "around." It's worth a try.

INDUSTRIAL vs GENERAL SALES

The sales to business are referred to as sales to organizational consumers. By far, most of the money transacted occurs here. This is to say that the highest dollar volume of sales is with organizational consumers.

Most people, when they think of sales, initially think of retail sales. You go into a store and you see a salesperson behind the counter, you make the purchase, and that's a retail sale. Another type of sale that is not called retail, but is a sale that is a brokerage type of sale is real estate. When you want to buy a house, you go to a real estate agent who acts as a broker between the seller and you, the purchaser. You have purchased the house from the seller but you have paid the real estate salesperson/broker a commission. In this section however, we are talking about sales from one company to another.

Let's take an example and discuss it. It's illustrated in Figure 3-1. Let's take a pharmaceutical product. Whether it's prescription or over-the-counter, is incidental. We can consider the over-the-counter type of product here.

The product we are discussing consists of a bottle of tablets. By the way, the pharmaceutical firms manufacture "tablets"—they don't make "pills." So if you are ever discussing anything with a pharmaceutical manufacturer don't refer to them as a pill-maker. Let's say the product is an antacid. The tablets are contained in a plastic bottle. There's a lot of cotton in the plastic bottle. There's a plastic cap on the plastic bottle. There's a label on the outside of the bottle. The bottle is packaged inside a cardboard box. The entire thing that we just mentioned is the product that you purchase when you purchase antacid tablets. Let's look in a little more detail about who bought what from whom to get you that product.

The tablets are manufactured by the pharmaceutical firm using chemicals that the firm purchased from a supplier. They mixed the ingredients or mixtures that they bought from an industrial supplier. They compressed, or manufactured, the tablets on machinery that they bought from another supplier. The tablets then traveled on a conveyor line that was purchased from another industrial supplier, before they were subsequently transferred into the plastic bottle.

The plastic bottle was purchased from another company. The company that sold the bottle made the bottle from plastic that it purchased from a plastics supplier. The plastics supplier made the plastics from other raw material chemicals that it purchased from a chemical supplier.

The cotton was purchased from a company that sells cotton.

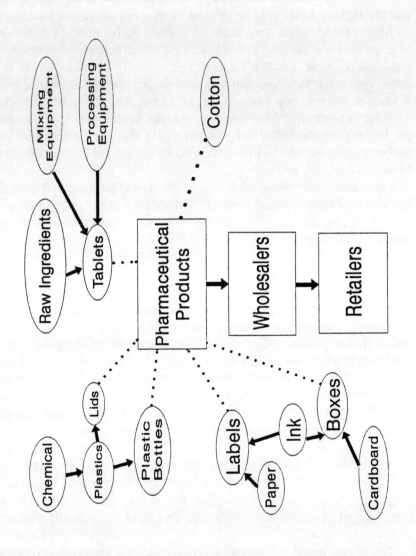

Figure 3-1.

The bottle cap may have been purchased from the same company that sold the bottle, or from another company.

The label was purchased from a label manufacturer. The label manufacturer purchased the paper and the ink from one or two different companies.

The box was purchased from a box supplier who printed the box using ink that it purchased from another company and the cardboard that it purchased from another company. Of course, this supplier also manufactured the cardboard using equipment that it purchased from another company.

Hopefully, this illustration will serve to show you some of the sales activity that takes place to bring a product to market, that is, to the retail market. There are wholesalers and distributors in the distribution chain that add to the dollar sales transaction. The bottles of antacid were sold to distributors and wholesalers in that chain of distribution before reaching the drugstore counter where you made the purchase.

You can figure this out for any of a number of products that are sold retail. If you consider an air conditioner, the air conditioner manufacturer purchased various metal parts from a supplier, then purchased the compressor from a company that manufactures compressors. The compressor company purchased the freon refrigerants from a chemical company, and so on.

There are other factors to be considered about industrial sales. Some things to remember about the organizational consumer, that is, the company the salesperson is selling to, are:

- Bidding and negotiations are relatively common here.
- Specifications are set up for the product purchased. In sales to federal and state governments, the specifications are very rigid.
- Industries acquire materials to use in further production. This was evident in the example just given.
- Many purchases are made through a purchasing department whose primary function is to make these purchases.
- There should be more logic and less emotion with industrial sales, whereas the reverse is many times true with retail sales.

If you are a salesperson of industrial products and you want to find your customers you can utilize the Standard Industrial Classification Index. The Office of Management and Budget of the government has classified businesses into various numerical categories. This classification system called the Standard Industrial Classification, S.I.C., categorizes major products, and hence the company that manufactures them, by a four digit code number. The number is referred to as the S.I.C. code.

The first two digits of the S.I.C. number show the major industrial group into which the company is classified. There are 10 divisions, which have a code range as follows:

01 to **09** Agriculture, forestry, and fishing
10 to **14** Mining
15 to **17** Construction
20 to **39** Manufacturing
40 to **49** Transportation, communication, electric, gas, and sanitary services
50 to **59** Wholesale and retail trade
60 to **67** Finance, insurance, and real estate
70 to **89** Services
91 to **97** Government
99 Nonclassifiable establishments

The last two digits of the S.I.C. code number classify the company more closely in its major group.

The pharmaceutical preparation that we discussed earlier, has the S.I.C. designation 2834. The 28 represents a manufacturing company and the 3 and the 4 get more and more specific.

This is a system similar to the Dewey decimal system used to categorize books in libraries. When you go into the library to look up a science book, you look up the 500 series and go that row of shelves. If it's a chemistry book you want to look up, you go the 530 section and then specifically if it's a physical chemistry book you go the 537 designation. This S.I.C. is very similar. It's a 4 digit code which gives many, many more variations and its an officially recognized code issued by the federal government.

Where do you find this information? Well, you go the library and then go to the reference section. If you are familiar with using the reference section, that's fine. If you are not, you'll now find that reference librarians are among the nicest people on earth. They like other people and they want to help them, and they are most helpful. You will find, or be directed to the Standard & Poors Register of Corporations, Directors and Executives. There are other books similar to this, but we'll talk about this one for now. This is a series of large books that contains a listing of major companies. These companies are listed, in one volume, in the numerical order of S.I.C. designation. In another volume, you can look up the companies alphabetically and then, as you read about the company—the corporate headquarters address, the officers names, annual sales, the type of business—you will see at the end of that write up the S.I.C. designation for that company.

If you know of one that you want to sell to, look up that company, find its S.I.C., and then look in the other volume under that S.I.C. and you'll find names of all the other companies that manufacture the same thing, and therefore would probably buy your product from you. One thing to watch out for here is that many of the larger companies have several S.I.C.s because they make a variety of products. Then just take a few more minutes to zero in on the companies that you want. Instead of just looking up one company and finding a single S.I.C., since you will possibly see 7 or 8 numbers for a given company, you may have to look up a few more companies and see which number is most common.

Many leading salespersons became leading salespersons by visiting the library, talking to the reference librarian, then making photocopies out of the Standard & Poors. Then they actively pursued and called on these companies and ended up with large sales volumes.

Incidentally, if you're job hunting, you will find that this book is very helpful to you in conducting your search, if you look at the type of company you want to join, find it's S.I.C., and then look at all the companies with that S.I.C., find out where they are located, the names of the officers of that company, and address your cover letters accordingly.

Compensation Methods

There are various ways of compensating a salesperson. Here, we won't discuss the exact dollars because that will vary from industry to industry and we would have to discuss rather wide ranges here. We will, however, mention the various "types" or methods that can be used to compensate a salesperson. They are:

- Straight salary
- Commission only
- Salary plus commission

Straight Salary

The straight salary method is very direct. This salesperson is not paid because of what amount he has sold. A salesperson who works for a company and is content to maintain existing accounts would be very content on a straight salary basis. Sometimes this person is also expected to generate new accounts while remaining on straight salary.

Commission Only

On the other hand, a real aggressive salesperson (aggressive in getting sales, not in personality) would rather work on a commission and get paid for new business generated. This is the type of person that says, "I can make your business grow. I can get you new accounts and expand the existing ones." This person would probably not be content with a straight salary and would want to be compensated for the new business.

Salary Plus Commission

The base salary plus commission is a combination that will provide a person with a base from which the normal ordinary business expenses can be met. Then, the commission is added onto this to compensate for the new sales generated.

Which of these methods a company uses depends on its product line, its particular stage of growth, and its goals especially in regard to sales. Many companies pick one of these methods and stick rigidly to it. There really is no reason however why a company can't have a combination of these methods available to salespersons as they progress through their careers with the company. You can start a person on a base salary and then, in time, as agreed upon by you and the person in your employ, switch them over to salary plus commission with the base salary being lower than the original salary situation, but with the existing commissions making up for that difference. If you are running a sales department, open up your thinking and find out what is best for the individual salespersons in your company. Don't worry about what the other salespersons will say about one person on a commission basis making a lot of money. If they're that good, then talk to them about switching over so they can also get wealthy.

Of course, automobiles can be company owned vehicles. They are worth several thousand dollars a year equivalent to salary.

The key here, as mentioned above, is to not restrict your thinking, but to keep your thoughts wide open and set up a compensation structure in your company in accordance with your existing product line, your current sales, and your goals.

SEGMENTATION: TERRITORIAL OR PRODUCT

This comparison is best made by giving an example. Let's say there are three salespersons, Charlie, Sally, and Ralph, in a sales department. Charlie sells product A throughout the entire United States. Sally sells product B throughout the entire Unites States, and Ralph sells product C throughout the entire United States. Your company, of course, manufactures products A, B, and C. Each person knows their product line inside out and is an expert in the field. Each person is running up large expenses with airline fares and hotel bills as they travel the entire United States selling their individual product line. It could be worthwhile to continue this way. On the other hand, let's discuss the situation that could occur. Suppose your company is based in New York and Charlie is in San Francisco selling product A. The customer says, "Charlie, I would like to talk to you about product B." Charlie has to say that he will have to go back and have Sally call on the phone since she is the specialist on product B. The customer says "Well, you're here, why can't you tell me?" Charlie explains that he can but it's really Sally's product and she's the expert. Now if you're the sales manager, you're beginning to see that it might be beneficial to have each of your three salespersons sell products A, B, and C, but you can't have them all traveling throughout the United States so, you think of switching from a product segmentation to a territorial segmentation. You rearrange the sales territories. Let's just roughly split the United States into 3 sections as Eastern, Central, and Western. Now, Charlie sells products A, B, and C in the Eastern part of the United States. Sally sells products A, B, and C in the Central part of the United States, and Ralph sells products A, B, and C in the Western part of the United States.

A very important thing to note here is that this is a major change! In addition to the customer getting used to new salespersons, maybe Charlie had a long established friendship with a particular customer in California and that person bought your product because Charlie sold it—not because of your company.

This doesn't happen you say? In several cases it does. Maybe also Charlie enjoyed taking his family on some of his trips to the West Coast. Now, it would be more expensive and he has to take them during his vacation time, since his activities are confined to the east coast.

Looking to the other side however, a particular customer may be glad that they can discuss products A, B, and C with one salesperson and, your airfares are reduced and the overall operating expense of the sales department is less than it was.

The key point here is to look at both methods and see which is best for your company, your customer, your product line, and your sales goals.

SALES FORECAST

The sales forecast is often not given the importance that it should have. The company budget should really be based on the sales forecast. Take yourself as an example. If you want to go on a cruise or some sort of expensive vacation next year, what do you usually do? Usually you'll say to yourself, "Well, I'm earning $XX this year and I expect to be working here next year and get a raise of X% and therefore I think I can take the cruise or the expensive vacation." What you're doing is calculating a future major expense and you're taking into account your current and projected income.

The same thing is done in business. The Chief Financial Officer, CFO, of the company, in order to plan the expenditures for next year wants to know the anticipated income for next year. This is represented by sales. The budget committee in allocating the funds for the company, which includes the allocations to the various departments within the company, wants to know the anticipated sales so that it can then plan the budget. Put quite simply, individual persons, or companies, in order to plan the expenditures, want to know what the probable income is going to be. The sales forecast tells just that for a company.

Generally, when you are getting ready to prepare your sales forecast you will have a graph or some presentation of data showing the sales occurring over the past five to ten years. You will look at this trend, and then take into consideration economic conditions that prevail at this time, great, wonderful new products that your company is going to put out onto the market that may boost sales a little extra, sales and marketing strategic planning to include the goals and then, let us not forget your "gut feeling" with regard to some customers that you feel are ready to buy more than they already are buying. These factors go into the sales forecast. It isn't as simple as some people think sometimes and just take the existing sales and multiply by 1.05. More thought should be given than that.

In addition to the budget, per se, there are other persons in various areas of the company who want to be aware of the forecast because, certain balance sheet items will vary with anticipated sales. Items such as receivables, inventory, and accounts payable to name a few, will change with varying sales. If sales are anticipated increasing significantly, then more inventories will have to be kept on hand, there will be a higher amount of receivables, and so on.

It is hoped that you now have a high level of respect for the sales forecast, if you did not have that high level before reading this.

SALES MANAGERS

Once a person becomes a sales manager, the responsibilities change from when that person was a salesperson. Quite often, a person with the highest amount of sales is promoted to sales manager when such an opening occurs. You may find some cases however where those that are on a commission structure want to stay on a commission structure and not be a sales manager. In cases where it's a strong, or 100% salary structure, the person with the highest sales is usually promoted to sales manager. He may not want to be a sales manager and may not be good at it, but the company figures that's the most likely person to be the next sales manager. With this person, *the toughest part of the new job is to have to stop doing the old job.* This person wants to "keep a few of my old accounts." I can't say that this should never be done because certainly in a few cases it could be appropriate. It would be in those cases where people are buying from "Charlie" and not so much from the company. In most cases however, the *new sales manager should manage the sales department and let the salespersons sell.* The new responsibilities include reviewing the territorial allocation, determining segmentation structure, hiring new salespersons, reporting to the vice president of sales and all those kinds of responsibilities.

The same is true in the science area where a chemist is really good and gets out a lot of technical publications and then, on that basis alone, is promoted to department head. If the bench chemist aspired to manage, his priority would be becoming department head and he would learn management techniques and be people oriented, then, that chemist will make a good department manager. In cases where a promotion was based only on the chemist with the highest number of publications, a real error was made. How do you prevent this? You set up a separate salary structure for the real producers and, if they have no interest in managing and don't want to manage then provide them with some additional compensation for the additional great work they are doing whether it's a chemist or a sales-person.

The main thing is very obvious now.   When you select a person to manage a department, make sure they have managerial abilities and stop them from doing their old job and make sure they do their new job.

CHAPTER 4

Finance

In days gone by this area enjoyed its own Ivory Tower, much like Research and Development sections did, and still do. Nowadays, with increasing costs and increasing opportunities, all department managers should be aware of the principles involved in order to run their own departments effectively, and, to be able to provide accurate cost and expense information to the financial managers of the company.

This is many times called Managerial Finance. You must remember that when you're a manager, everything is managerial something...managerial train commuting, managerial golf, managerial napping, managerial lunch, etc.

The topics that will be covered are:

— Management's Primary Goal
— Depreciation
— Debt & Equity, Interest & Dividends
— The Time Value of money (The single most important concept in Finance)
  • Present Value
  • Future Value
— Bond Valuation
— Stock Valuation
— Expected Value
— Economies of Scale and Diminishing Returns
— Financial Statements
  • Profit and Loss Statement, Income Statement
  • Balance Sheet

— Retained Earnings
— Ratio Analysis
— Capital Budgeting
  • Payback Period
  • Net Present Value
  • Internal Rate of Return
— Cash Flow Analysis
— Operating Leverage
— Risk and Rates of return

Now we will venture into the world of Finance. *Many of the things we will discuss will apply to you in decisions that you make in life, every day—here they are simply on a larger monetary scale, and apply to your company.*

MANAGEMENT'S PRIMARY GOAL

Management's primary goal is to maximize shareholder wealth, pure and simple. You do this by running the company so well that the common stock is in demand and the price of the stock goes up.

In the case of a sole proprietorship the owner strives to make as much profit as possible. What's possible? Keep raising the prices until your customers find it worth their while to purchase from your competitor whereas before you raised your prices they bought from you. The market thus determines what your maximum will be.

In the case of a corporation, the shareholders, (i.e., stockholders) are the owners and it is their wealth that is to be maximized. How will you really know that the value of the stock has been maximized? Well, you really won't, but you'll believe that you came close. For example, if stock, in your first year as president, rose from $20 to $30 per share and you think that that's great, people can always say that it should have gone to $32. You will have done well and you can believe that you "maximized" the value at $30.

DEPRECIATION

The things that you want to know about depreciation are that it is non-cash and that it is an expense item. This is to say that depreciation is a non-cash expense! Since it's an expense, it is a tax deduction. Since it's a non-cash item, a Financial Manager looks at it differently than an

Accountant. The latter lists this in the appropriate records such as the Income Statement and the Balance Sheet while the former is primarily interested in cash flows on the premise that cash flows determine how well the business is going.

The Financial Manager realizes that, as a tax deduction, depreciation reduces Net Operating Income (which is Earnings Before Interest and Taxes, which is EBIT), and thereby reduces the amount of taxes that the company must pay. This, of course, is good, but it doesn't show how well the company is being run...especially if much of what is being depreciated was purchased years ago (maybe when the company was being run by someone else). The cash flows are what determine how the company is running now.

Congress changes the permissible tax depreciation methods every so often. In 1981, previous methods were replaced by a method called the Accelerate Cost Recovery System (ACRS, and pronounced acres). The system was changed by the Tax Reform Act of 1988. It retained its ACRS name. The asset lives permitted are listed in Table 4-1.

DEBT AND EQUITY

Interest and Dividends

Debt and Equity are the two methods used to finance an enterprise. The easiest way to remember these is to keep in mind the following:

DEBT   - Bonds; you still control the business, you make periodic interest payments to the bondholders, and then you pay back the original numerical value to those persons. They don't tell you how to run the company.

EQUITY - Stock; you have sold a "piece of the action," you may choose to pay dividends at times. Since the common stockholders are part owners of the business, they can tell you how to run the company.

Now, let's say more about each of these.

Stocks and Bonds

Generally, when we talk about stocks, we will be talking about common stock. The value of the company, i.e., the company's worth, is always

Table 4-1. Classes and Asset Lives assigned through the 1986 TAX REFORM ACT

Class	Property
3 year	Computers and Research Equipment
5 year	Cars, various vehicles, some computers
7 year	Office furniture and fixtures, most industrial equipment
10 year	Some industrial equipment
27.5 year	Residential real property
31.5 year	Nonresidential real property, i.e., commercial and industrial buildings

referred to in terms of the common stock. This is good to keep in mind as you learn more and more about the business of business. There are various classes of stock and there is preferred stock. Preferred stock is referred to as a "hybrid," in the sense that it is considered by some to be somewhere in between a bond and a share of common stock. More about preferred stock later in this chapter.

When you, the company, issue shares of common stock, you are selling away a "piece of the action." Persons who purchase the stock are purchasing that stock for two reasons, both of which refer to their income. The first is that they want the company to increase in value, and therefore the stock will increase in value, and their stock will be worth more to them to keep or sell at a profit. This is called capital gains. The second income source is the dividend payout by the company to the shareholders. A company does not have to pay dividends to the shareholders. It chooses to do this. When a company has computed its sales for the year, and then subtracted from that its expenses like the cost of sales, interest, payments, taxes, etc., what remains is called net income—more specifically, net income available to common shareholders. This income can now be divided two ways: it can be plowed back into the business or it can be given as dividends to the shareholders. When it is plowed back into the business, it is called retained earnings. This is a misnomer. The retained earnings are not really retained in a drawer or a file cabinet. This refers to those earnings that are used to reinvest in the business, i.e., they are used to hire more people or purchase new machinery, etc., for the business. The dividends of course are given to the common shareholders.

Some companies have never paid dividends but have chosen to reinvest everything in retained earnings, which is, putting the money back into the business. In those cases, the shareholders are looking only for capital gains increase since they will not be receiving dividends. In the case however, of a company that has provided dividends, say on a quarterly basis, for a number of years, it would be psychologically unwise to not pay dividends in a particular quarter of a year or end of a year in order to put the money back into the business. This is true even if the company has excellent investment opportunities. The reason for this is really very simple. On paper, while it looks like the company can make great strides forward by not paying dividends and therefore reinvesting all the profits back into the business, you should picture this from the shareholders point of view. Let's say the company has been paying dividends quarterly for the last ten years, That's 40 consecutive dividends. Now, the company chooses not to pay dividends but to reinvest the money in the business along with that normal portion of retained earnings. Picture this as a shareholder who is not intimately involved in the running of the business. This shareholder is not a vice president, or a director or whatever. This shareholder is a regular investor. Is the shareholder really going to believe that you have great investment opportunities or is he going to think that something has gone wrong and that you need the money for something else? In most cases, the shareholders will begin to wonder what has gone awry, and this is why, psychologically, it is unwise after having paid a string of dividends, to not pay a dividend for a particular quarter or a year. The confidence of the shareholders goes down, they begin to sell their stock, and the price of the stock goes down, and therefore, the value of the firm goes down. So you see, even though there may be an excellent investment opportunity, a company that has routinely paid dividends would be wise to pay some sort of dividend.

There is another way to go about this. A company can chose to take all the money and invest it back into the business and can issue a stock dividend. Now, the company has "retained" the money and reinvested it, and at the same time the shareholders are happy because they received a dividend. This is easier said than done and it would be unwise to try this more than one single time or the same thing as described above will happen.

When bonds are issued, they are issued with the promise of paying interest, and the interest that is paid is normally higher than the dividend rate. For example, a dividend, calculated over a year, whether it is paid once in that year or whether it is paid four times (quarterly) during that year, can be say 6, 8, or 10%. The interest rate on a bond might be 15%.

Why is there this difference? Well, there are a couple of factors. A primary factor here is that the interest paid on a bond is a tax deduction. The dividend is not. The dividend is paid after taxes have been paid to the government. Therefore, when a company pays an interest rate of 15% on a bond, it would have had to pay much of that money to the government in taxes had it not issued the bond and made the promise of payment, so therefore, the "effective" interest payment can be looked upon at being less than 15%. The other reason that you are willing to pay a little more to the bondholder is because the bondholder doesn't have any say in how you run the company. The bondholder is not an owner of the company. The bondholder is an investor, but does not have any control over how you run the company. The shareholder does.

Let's take a typical bond and we'll say a thousand dollar bond with a term of ten years and an annual interest rate of 15%. In this case, the purchaser of the bond buys it from the company—through underwriters—for $1,000. You, the company, will pay that person $150 (that's 15% of one thousand) each year for the next ten years, and at the end of the tenth year when you pay that tenth payment of $150 you will also then give the $1,000 back to the bondholder. Of course, keep in mind that these bonds can be sold from investor to investor, usually through brokers in the market and that this example is simply saying that if one particular person held the bond this is what the person would receive. You, the company, still have to pay it regardless of who holds the bond at the time of the payment. It seems like the company is paying $2,500 for $1,000, and on paper, it is. That's 10 × 150 which equals 1,500 plus the original 1,000. However, since the value of money decreases in time, the second year's $150 is not worth $150 and the third year's $150 payment is worth even less than that and so on and so forth. This is covered in discounted cash flow later in this chapter. Then, when the tenth year is up and the $1,000 payment is made, that $1,000 is not worth nearly that in today's dollars. So in actuality, the value of the bond will still be $1,000 in terms of today's dollars—something that can be shown in discounted cash flow analysis.

In the case that we just described, the term of the bond was ten years and the yield was 15%.

There are all sorts of variations on this theme. There are convertible bonds, which are bonds that can be converted to stock or whatever at some subsequent time at some subsequent value. In the case of a convertible bond, the conditions would be specified such as "one bond can be converted into XX shares of such and such stock at a price of $Y. This is good until such and such date."

Preferred stock is a hybrid. It is called this in the sense that it's stock by the definition of stock; however, the point to be made here is that the name seems appropriate: it is "preferred" and those shareholders are preferred shareholders. This is said for more than one reason. First, dividends are always paid to holders of preferred stock. This is not a "have to" by law but it is a "have to" by tradition, and encourages people to buy preferred stock. The other advantage to this is that it ranks higher than common stock as a security issue. This is to say that if a company had to liquidate it's assets, the bondholders would be the first in line to get paid on the sale of those assets, then the preferred shareholders would get their money, and the common shareholders would be last in line. In fact, if the company is ever in deep enough trouble to have to liquidate, then, usually, it is in such deep trouble that there is nothing left for the common shareholders. If there was enough for everyone in the first place, the company would not be in trouble.

Hopefully, now you see the differences between bonds and preferred stock and common stock.

What's the difference between bonds and stocks from the investors' point of view? This is a matter of the investors' personal preference. Does the investor want the guaranteed income (yield, interest payments) and the security of knowing what that payment is going to be each year or does the investor want the capital gains and the likely dividend payments and the ownership and voting rights of the common shareholder? This is what will make the difference for the investor.

What difference does it make from the company's point of view? Do you, the company, want to have other people controlling the company such as would be the case if you issued common stock? On the other hand, you don't have to pay dividends when you issue common stock. You have not promised dividends like you promised interest payments on a bond. You can choose to issue bonds and therefore make a promise to pay an interest payment every year along with the original numerical value of the bond at the end of the term and relax in that you know that the investors don't have a say in the running of your company. Another factor comes into play after your first issue of stocks or bonds is on the market. If you have chosen to issue stock initially, and then a few years later need more money for expansion, it may be advisable to use the debt mechanism of bonds so you don't dilute the company too much with the stock. On the other hand, if you have a bond issue on the market, you may find it wise to issue stock instead of more bonds because, since you have bonds out there already, another bond issue would be considered more risky and would therefore carry a higher yield. So you see, in order to put one bond issue behind another that's already out there, the world recognizes that you are already obligated to make payments to the existing bondholders and says, in effect, "since you have that obligation, I consider this more risky and, therefore, I want a higher interest payment if I am going to loan you my money."

You see, while there are many variations on the themes that have just been discussed, the rationale behind these issues is really quite simple, and this rationale applies to all firms regardless of how many issues and how seemingly complex they are.

THE TIME VALUE OF MONEY

The Single Most Important Concept in Finance

The concept of the time value of money simply means that you take money spent or received at a time in the past or at a time in the future and you equate that to today. Alternatively, you can take money spent or received in the past or spent or received now, and equate that to what it will be worth at some point in the future.

In business, when you get into long range planning, you will be considering an investment to be made today or maybe next year and you will look at the anticipated returns perhaps five years from now. When you anticipate a particular dollar value return say, five years from now, you are interested in what that amount of money would be worth today or the day you make the investment. This permits a better evaluation of different projects. All projects don't start producing their cash inflow at the same time, however, when you equate them to today's dollars you now have a basis for a comparison. This is what you call bringing things to their Present Value. When you do the reverse of this and equate things to what they will be equal to at a particular point in the future you call that Future Value. What happens when you are equating something in the past? Well, there are two things to consider here. First, the past is done and there is nothing you can do about it except learn from it. Secondly, if you do equate something in the past, you will still refer to the starting date of an investment as Present Value and you will refer to the ending time period of your consideration as your Future Value.

Here is a key factor in the understanding of the time value of money. When you evaluate investments, the Present Value refers to the starting value of the investment, whenever that occurred or will occur and, the Future Value refers to the ending value whenever that occurred or will occur.

Table 4-2. Compound Interest Calculations

Year	Amount at Beginning of Year, $PV \times (1 + k) = $ Amount at End of Year, FV_n	Interest Earned, $PV(k)$
1	$100.00 \times 1.07 = \$107.00$	\$ 7.00
2	$107.00 \times 1.07 = \ \ 114.49$	7.49
3	$114.49 \times 1.07 = \ \ 122.50$	8.01
4	$122.50 \times 1.07 = \ \ 131.08$	8.58
5	$131.08 \times 1.07 = \ \ 140.26$	9.18
		$\overline{\$40.26}$

For example, if you are planning on making an investment next year and the "term" over which you are going to evaluate this is three years, then, the Present Value is the value that the money will have next year, that is one year from now, and, the Future Value is the value the investment will have four years from now, i.e., at the end of the three year term. If you keep this in mind you won't go wrong—the Present Value is the starting value of the investment and the Future Value is the ending of the investment regardless of when the investment commenced.

When we are calculating what the value will be in the future, we generally call that *compounding*. When we calculate in the other direction, we call that *discounting*. Let's take a look at an example of compounding and we'll see what we mean.

Let's say that you had $100 and you want to put that $100 in the bank and you were told by the bank that the interest rate is 7%. First, you want to check to see if that's simple interest or compound interest, because, if you are going to leave that in the bank for five years and the return is simple interest, you will get $7 on that $100 for each of the five years giving you a total of $35 interest and a grand total of $135 in your account. On the other hand, with compound interest, the sequence would be different. At the end of the first year, your $100 would have gained $7 giving you $107; at the end of the second year, the $107 would gain 7% and you would get $7.49 on that $107. Now during the third year, you have the $100 plus the $7 plus the $7.49 sitting in your account and you will get $8.01 interest on that, and so on and so forth as illustrated in Table

4-2. So you see, at the end of five years, you have gained $40.26 interest and now have a total of $140.26 in your account.

You may say that "That is only $5.26 more than the $135 I would have had with simple interest." Well, your goal is to maximize profit so therefore, you should always go for the higher value. Note that when you compare $40.26 to $35.00, the $40.26 is 15% greater than the $35.00. Additionally, as the interest rates, or a rate of return on an investment increase and go beyond 7% to 14%, 18%, 25%, etc., these differences become greatly magnified. Another factor to consider is that you are not talking about $100 with your business. You're talking millions of dollars. So, when you're talking millions of dollars and rates of return on investments around 20%, 25%, or 30%, the values are very significant.

Take a look at this mathematically. Setting this up in an equation form we have:

PV = present value of your account, or the beginning amount, $100.

k = interest rate the bank pays you = 7% per year, or expressed as a decimal, 0.07. On financial calculators, the term i is frequently used rather than k.

I = dollars of interest you earn during the year = k(PV).

FV_n = future value, or ending amount, of your account at the end of n years. Whereas PV is the value now, at the *present* time, FV_n is the value n years into the future after compound interest has been earned. Note also that FV_0 is the future value *zero* years into the future, which is the *present*, so FV_0 = PV.

n = number of years, or, more generally, periods, involved in the investment.

In our example, n = 1, so FV_n = FV_1, calculated as follows:

$$
\begin{aligned}
FV_1 &= PV + I \\
&= PV + PV(k) \\
&= PV(1 + k)
\end{aligned}
\tag{4-1}
$$

In words, the *Future Value, FV,* at the end of one period is the Present Value times the quantity 1 plus the interest rate.

We can now use Equation 4-1 to find how much your $100 will be worth at the end of one year at a 7% interest rate:

$$FV_1 = \$100(1 + 0.07) = \$100(1.07) = \$107$$

Your account will earn $7 of interest (I = $7), so you will have $107 at the end of the year.

Now, as we stretch out to the equation taking into account each of the five years in our example, we get the following:

$$
\begin{aligned}
FV_5 &= PV(1 + k)(1 + k)(1 + k)(1 + k)(1 +k) \\
&= PV(1 + k)^5 \\
&= PV(1 + .07)^5 \\
&= PV(1.07)^5 \\
&= PV(1.4026)
\end{aligned}
$$

Instead of doing that somewhat lengthy calculation each time, we can actually set up a chart. We can have what we will call a future value interest factor, FVIF, calculated for various combinations of time periods and percentages and then, when we see a combination of time period and percentage rate of return, we can simply refer to the chart and use that factor. Actually, nowadays there are computer programs that have this all set into them and, many of the smaller calculators that you carry in your attache case are programmable to this. However, this chart may not only be convenient, it will serve to show you just what's going on in this type of calculation (see Table 4-3).

The table is set up for a value of $1 therefore, when you set your present value equal to a number of dollars you simply multiply that number of dollars by the factor for $1 and you get your answer.

Another significant item here is that we talk in terms of *periods.* The reason we do this is that not all periods are equated to years. For example, in our illustration of 7% over five years, if that were presented as with semi-annual compounding, then there would be ten compounding periods and n would equal 10. At the same time, since compounding was semi-annual and the interest rate was quoted as an annual interest rate of 7% the actual interest rate, or rate of return, k, would be 3.5%. So you see, pay

Table 4-3. Future Value of $1 at the End of n Periods

$$FVIF_{k,n} = (1 + k)^n$$

Period (n)	1%	2%	3%	4%	5%	6%	7%	8%	9%	10%
1	1.0100	1.0200	1.0300	1.0400	1.0500	1.0600	1.0700	1.0800	1.0900	1.1000
2	1.0201	1.0404	1.0609	1.0816	1.1025	1.1236	1.1449	1.1664	1.1881	1.2100
3	1.0303	1.0612	1.0927	1.1249	1.1576	1.1910	1.2250	1.2597	1.2950	1.3310
4	1.0406	1.0824	1.1255	1.1699	1.2155	1.2625	1.3108	1.3605	1.4116	1.4641
5	1.0510	1.1041	1.1593	1.2167	1.2763	1.3382	1.4026	1.4693	1.5386	1.6105
6	1.0615	1.1262	1.1941	1.2653	1.3401	1.4185	1.5007	1.5869	1.6771	1.7716
7	1.0721	1.1487	1.2299	1.3159	1.4071	1.5036	1.6058	1.7138	1.8280	1.9487
8	1.0829	1.1717	1.2668	1.3686	1.4775	1.5938	1.7182	1.8509	1.9926	2.1436
9	1.0937	1.1951	1.3048	1.4233	1.5513	1.6895	1.8385	1.9990	2.1719	2.3579
10	1.1046	1.2190	1.3439	1.4802	1.6289	1.7908	1.9672	2.1589	2.3674	2.5937

careful attention to how the interest rate or rate of return is quoted and adjust if necessary for the time period. Additionally, pay strict attention to the compounding and adapt accordingly.

Let's take an example of this particular thing. If you were considering a situation that was going to have a return of 12% annual and a term of five years and the compounding was quarterly, then, while the number of years is 5, the number of periods is

$$5 \times 4 = 20$$

At the same time, since the interest rate was quoted as 12% annual, that interest rate will be $1/4 \times 12$ which equals 3%. So here you would have $n = 20$ and $k = 3$. It makes a big difference!

Discounting is the reverse of compounding. While we say it's the *reverse* of compounding, mathematically it's the *inverse* of compounding. What you are saying is if I have so many dollars that I want to receive in the future, and the rate of return is such and such, how many dollars must I have available to invest today? Here, we are taking the Future Value and we will know the rate of return and the number of compounding periods and we will calculate the Present Value. We are going to take Equation 4-1 and then rearrange it. Remember, Equation 4-1 was $FV = PV (1 + k)$. When solving for PV we divide both sides through by $(1 + k)$ and we get

$$PV = \frac{FV_n}{(1 + k)^n} = FV_n(1 + k)^{-n} = FV_n \left(\frac{1}{1 + k}\right)^n \qquad (4\text{-}2)$$

From Equation 4-2, you see what we mean when we say that discounting, or going from future value back to present value is the inverse of compounding. Here again we can make various calculations and set up a table. In fact, we have done this, and the values of the Present Value Interest Factor, PVIF, for $1 are shown in that table. (See Table 4-4.)

Look at this, using the same details as in our compounding example, as though we are asking ourselves the question, "If I can get a rate of return on investment of 7% compounded annually for five years and I want to earn $140.26, how much will I have to invest now to do that?" and that is explained here

$$PV = FV_5(PVIF_{7\%,\ 5\ years})$$
$$= 140.26(0.7130)$$
$$= \$100$$

This example contained our previous data and therefore worked out to precisely $100. Of course, in real life you may be saying something like "If I want $100,000 in 3 years and I can have annual compounding with an annual interest rate of 10% how much must I invest now?" In this case, you would look in Table 4-4 and when you see 3 compounding periods at 10% the figure would be 0.7513 and, 0.7513 × $100,000 = $75,130. That's the amount you would have to invest now at 10% compounded annually to have a total of $100,000 in 3 years.

Another key point to remember any time you have a problem such as this to work out, is that you are always dealing with four things. These things are the Present Value, the Future Value, the rate of return, and the number of periods. When you know any three you can always calculate the fourth. If you only know two you can't calculate the third and fourth. You need more information. You must know three things to calculate the fourth.

How do you calculate the interest rate? Well, if you know the Present Value and the Future Value you can divide the Present Value by the Future Value and obtain the Present Value interest factor. Now, with the Present Value interest factor and the number of periods you look in the chart and find the rates and find k. In fact, you can do this two ways. If you choose to divide the Present Value by the Future Value, you will get the Present Value Interest Factor and you will look up k on the Present Value Interest Factor table. If you choose to divide the Future Value by the Present Value, you will get the Future Value Interest Factor and you can look up, knowing the number of periods, the rate, k in the Future Value interest table.

Another important point is something that will prevent you from making an error that many people make. Remember, when you are talking about the future you are always wanting your money to grow so your Future Value Interest Factor is going to be greater than 1. When you're calculating Present Value, you are looking for an investment figure that is smaller than what you have now (now meaning the future) and that number, the Present Value Interest Value, PVIF, will be less than one. This may sound simple enough, but a great percentage of people look in the wrong table and do a calculation going in the wrong direction! When you are

Table 4-4. Present Value of $1 Due at the End of n Periods

$$PVIF_{k,n} = \frac{1}{(1 + k)^n} = \left(\frac{1}{1 + k}\right)^n$$

Period (n)	1%	2%	3%	4%	5%	6%	7%	8%	9%	10%
1	.9901	.9804	.9709	.9615	.9524	.9434	.9346	.9259	.9174	.9091
2	.9803	.9612	.9426	.9246	.9070	.8900	.8734	.8573	.8417	.8264
3	.9706	.9423	.9151	.8890	.8638	.8396	.8163	.7938	.7722	.7513
4	.9610	.9238	.8885	.8548	.8227	.7921	.7629	.7350	.7084	.6830
5	.9515	.9057	.8626	.8219	.7835	.7473	.7130	.6806	.6499	.6209
6	.9420	.8880	.8375	.7903	.7462	.7050	.6663	.6302	.5963	.5645
7	.9327	.8706	.8131	.7599	.7107	.6651	.6227	.5835	.5470	.5132
8	.9235	.8535	.7894	.7307	.6768	.6274	.5820	.5403	.5019	.4665
9	.9143	.8368	.7664	.7026	.6446	.5919	.5439	.5002	.4604	.4241
10	.9053	.8203	.7441	.6756	.6139	.5584	.5083	.4632	.4224	.3855

Table 4-5. Future Value of an Annuity of $1 per Period for n Periods

$$FVIFA_{k,n} = \sum_{t=1}^{n} (1 + k)^{n-t} = \frac{(1 + k)^n - 1}{k}$$

Number of Periods (n)	1%	2%	3%	4%	5%	6%	7%	8%	9%	10%
1	1.0000	1.0000	1.0000	1.0000	1.0000	1.0000	1.0000	1.0000	1.0000	1.0000
2	2.0100	2.0200	2.0300	2.0400	2.0500	2.0600	2.0700	2.0800	2.0900	2.1000
3	3.0301	3.0604	3.0909	3.1216	3.1525	3.1836	3.2149	3.2464	3.2781	3.3100
4	4.0604	4.1216	4.1836	4.2465	4.3101	4.3746	4.4399	4.5061	4.5731	4.6410
5	5.1010	5.2040	5.3091	5.4163	5.5256	5.6371	5.7507	5.8666	5.9847	6.1051
6	6.1520	6.3081	6.4684	6.6330	6.8019	6.9753	7.1533	7.3359	7.5233	7.7156
7	7.2135	7.4343	7.6625	7.8983	8.1420	8.3938	8.6540	8.9228	9.2004	9.4872
8	8.2857	8.5830	8.8923	9.2142	9.5491	9.8975	10.2598	10.6366	11.0285	11.4359
9	9.3685	9.7546	10.1591	10.5828	11.0266	11.4913	11.9780	12.4876	13.0210	13.5795
10	10.4622	10.9497	11.4639	12.0061	12.5779	13.1808	13.8164	14.4866	15.1929	15.9374

Table 4-6. Present Value of an Annuity of $1 per Period for n Periods

$$PVIFA_{k,n} = \sum_{t=1}^{n} \frac{1}{(1+k)^t} = \frac{1 - \dfrac{1}{(1+k)^n}}{k} = \frac{1}{k} - \frac{1}{k(1+k)^n}$$

Number of Periods (n)	1%	2%	3%	4%	5%	6%	7%	8%	9%	10%
1	0.9901	0.9804	0.9709	0.9615	0.9524	0.9434	0.9346	0.9259	0.9174	0.9091
2	1.9704	1.9416	1.9135	1.8861	1.8594	1.8334	1.8080	1.7833	1.7591	1.7355
3	2.9410	2.8839	2.8286	2.7751	2.7232	2.6730	2.6243	2.5771	2.5313	2.4869
4	3.9020	3.8077	3.7171	3.6299	3.5460	3.4651	3.3872	3.3121	3.2397	3.1699
5	4.8534	4.7135	4.5797	4.4518	4.3295	4.2124	4.1002	3.9927	3.8897	3.7908
6	5.7955	5.6014	5.4172	5.2421	5.0757	4.9173	4.7665	4.6229	4.4859	4.3553
7	6.7282	6.4720	6.2303	6.0021	5.7864	5.5824	5.3893	5.2064	5.0330	4.8684
8	7.6517	7.3255	7.0197	6.7327	6.4632	6.2098	5.9713	5.7466	5.5348	5.3349
9	8.5660	8.1622	7.7861	7.4353	7.1078	6.8017	6.5152	6.2469	5.9952	5.7590
10	9.4713	8.9826	8.5302	8.1109	7.7217	7.3601	7.0236	6.7101	6.4177	6.1446

calculating a Future Value, your Future Value Interest Factor is greater than 1. When you are calculating a Present Value, your Present Value Interest Factor is smaller than 1.

An annuity is a series of regular payments. This series of payments extends for a finite period of time. There are two types of annuities: one in which the payment is made at the beginning of the time period, and the other in which the payment is made at the end of the time period. The latter is the most common and that will be the type referred to here. The same principle applies to calculating either one—you simply shift the time frame because the payments are made earlier in one than the other. Here, however, we will consider the annuities where the payments are made at the end of the time period. As with the individual lump sum payments, we can have Present Value and we can have Future Value. Here, we have elected to simply present the charts and you can see that Table 4-5 shows the chart for the Future Value of an annuity of $1 per period or n periods. Table 4-6 shows a Present Value of an annuity of $1 per period or n periods. Note that here what we said about the Present Value factor being smaller than 1 in all cases does not hold. The reason it doesn't hold is that we are talking about an annuity which is a *series* of regular payments at regular time intervals.

What if you have a series that is either not regular in time or not regular in amount invested? Then, you don't have an annuity. You have several individual Present Value or Future Value problems to be solved individually and then combined. That's the way it is!

This concept of discounted cash flow, which is the general term applied to the compounding and discounting processes will come into play throughout your business calculations. I stated at the beginning of this section that it was *the single most important concept in managerial finance,* and I hope that as you see its application to some of the problems that you may now be facing in your business and other situations as you progress through this book, you will realize how important it is.

BOND VALUATION

We have already mentioned that the payment on a bond is comprised of a series of regular, usually annual, payments of interest plus at the end of the term, the repayment of the original numerical price of the bond. Therefore, if for example, you had purchased a $1,000, 15% annual, ten year term bond, and you were the holder of that bond, you would have given the issuer $1,000 at the very beginning, and then at the end of the first year you would receive from the issuer $150, and at the end of the second year you would receive another $150, and at the end of the third year you would receive another $150, and so on and so forth until the end of the tenth year at which time you would receive $150 plus your $1,000 back. You see here that this source of funds back to you can be looked upon as two different sources. The $150 (in this case) is given to you at the end of each year for ten years, therefore, you have a regular series of payments made to you at regular time intervals, and therefore you have an annuity. You also have the original $1,000 returned to you at the end of the ten years, but, this $1,000 ten years from now is not equal to $1,000 today. What you have here in valuing the bond is a discounted cash flow calculation that is really the sum of two different cash flow problems. Look now at the equation used to find a bond's value

$$\text{Value} = V = \text{the sum of } I\left(\frac{1}{1+k}\right)^t + M\left(\frac{1}{1+k}\right)^n =$$

$$= I(\text{PVIFA}_{k,n}) + M(\text{PVIF}_{k,n})$$

where:

I = amount of interest paid each period

M = par value, or maturity value, which in this case was $1,000

k = rate of interest on the bond

n = number of payment periods until the bond matures

t = the time period of the annuity

Typically, when the annuity is discounted and the lump sum payment is discounted, the grand total will equal the original value of the bond. In this case, even though $10 \times 150 = \$1,500$, plus the $1,000 equals $2,500, when all this is discounted back to terms of today's dollars, the value will amount to $1,000 in this case. Note also that the calculation is simplified by using for the annuity the PVIFA, Present Value Interest Factor for an Annuity from the tables, and the factor for discounting the lump sum payment is the Present Value Interest Factor, PVIF, for a lump sum payment which can be found from its appropriate table.

So you see, the calculation, although representing two different mechanisms, is not difficult at all.

Now, in real life, bonds are sold from one holder through the market, to another holder. Well, the way you determine the value of a bond at that time is to use a suitable factor n for the number of years remaining on the bond. For example, if a ten year term bond is sold from one bondholder to another bondholder after four years, the value of the bond is determined by calculating using the same equations but letting n equal the remaining six years. Then when you look up the PVIFA and the PVIF in their suitable tables you use n equal to 6. This then will give you a suitable value to use for the sale or purchase for the bond at that point in time.

STOCK VALUATION

Common stocks are valued by looking at two sources of gain for the stock. The person buying the stock will see income from two sources. Those sources are the dividend yield plus the actual gain in value of the share of stock. So, if you purchase a share of stock you are usually hoping to receive a dividend, and at the same time, to have that stock gain in value as the firm gains in value. In equation form, this is represented as:

$$\begin{array}{ccccc} \text{Expected Rate} & = & \text{Expected} & + & \text{Expected Growth} \\ \text{of Return} & & \text{Dividend} & & \text{Rate or Capital} \\ & & \text{Yield} & & \text{Gains Yield} \end{array}$$

$$k \quad = \quad \frac{D}{P} \quad + \quad g$$

where:

D = amount of dividend per share
P = price paid for a share

Here, as with bonds, we have two mechanisms by which the value of the stock will increase. The difference between this and bonds is that this is not discounted and the reason it is not discounted is because we are speaking of a rate of return and not an absolute number. In the case of the bond, we were talking about an individual price of the bond and therefore we discounted our figures. Here, in the case of a common stock, we value this by computing a rate of return, more correctly called an expected rate of return, and therefore, there is no need to discount the values used. It is significant though to keep the similarities in mind.

The market price of the stock should parallel the growth of the company and the value of the company. Generally, this does occur although, depending on the industry, there is sometimes a time lag between the growth of the value of the company and the increase in the market price of the stock.

Then, we have some cases where the companies will not grow but will pay a constant stream of dividends. Some utility companies are like this. They may serve a relatively small community and, they will not have a growth rate but they pay dividends routinely. How do you value these stocks? Use the same equation but keep in mind that g = 0. The equation then reduces to calculating your dividend rate.

EXPECTED VALUE

There is a term called Expected Value which is used in stock and bond valuation which really means the expected return on those.   There is another term called Expected Value which is a separate thing. You will know when each is being used by the way it is used. For example, when someone wants you to find the expected value of a bond, then you use the term associated with bond valuation. If, however, you are going to evaluate alternative investments based on the *expected value* of the return, then you will be using what is going to be described here. The expected value of a project is the possible return on the project multiplied by the probability that it will occur. An example can best illustrate this. Suppose you had three different projects—A, B, and C—and you could select only one of these projects, i.e., they are mutually exclusive. You can choose whichever one you want but you can't select more than one. You know a particular amount associated with the return on each project and you know the probability that the return will occur. For example, project A has a 50% probability of returning $100,000. The other 50% represents a zero return. There is no in between. Project B has a 20% probability that it will return $120,000 to you. As before, it will either return this or it will return nothing. Project C has a 30% probability of returning $150,000 to you.

If you select these on the basis of the return, you will select Project C because it has the largest potential return, $150,000. However, there is only a 30% probability that it will occur. Keeping in mind that the probabilities have to total 100%, we see that A and B total the other 70%. When you multiply the return by the probability of occurrence, for instance, multiplying for project A, 0.5 × $100,000, you get an expected value of $50,000 and so on and so forth. So you see, when you take the probability of occurrence times the anticipated return (if, in fact, the project were to be successful at all), the number that you get is called the Expected Value. Remember, you will never actually realize this exact number. It's only a mathematical expression representing a function of the probability of the return if it comes in. You see project A will give you either $100,000 or zero. It will not give you $50,000. However, $50,000 represents the term that is called Expected Value and when you calculate the Expected Value for each project, you have a basis for comparison.

This is used by some people to select which project to pursue. There are many other people who don't care to use this method at all. It is not presented here as a recommended procedure. It is described so that you will know that it is an alternative method by which you can view relationships between various projects. In actuality, the term Expected Value is a misnomer since it is a value that you will not attain. However, it's like a tool in your tool box. You can use it if you want or you can choose not to use it. But you know that it is in the toolbox. (See Table 4-7.)

ECONOMIES OF SCALE

This is a term used to indicate that as the quantity or production of a particular thing increases, the incremental cost decreases. As an example of this, let's say that you are ordering letterhead sheets of paper from a printer. The printer will tell you that it will cost $125 for 1,000 sheets. When you ask how much for 2,000 sheets the printer says $160 and you quickly calculate and find that it was only $35 for the second 1,000. This continues on with larger quantities as indicated in Table 4-8. As you see in the table, when you get to larger quantities, the cost per thousand, i.e., the incremental cost per thousand decreases. The right hand column of the table shows the average cost and, of course, that will also decrease with larger quantities if the incremental cost decreases.

What factors contribute to this? Well, the reason the first thousand cost so much is because the printer had to set up the printing press for your letterhead. That's a fixed cost that will not be repeated with any increase in number of copies. Next, the printer had to mix the right inks to get the

Table 4-7. Expected Value

Project	Probability of Occurrence	Return	Expected Value
A	50%	$100,000	$50,000
B	20%	$120,000	$24,000
C	30%	$150,000	$45,000

color you wanted. Then, the printer had to order a minimum quantity of paper in the color and texture that you wanted, and, when you order 1,000 copies, the printer might have 9,000 sheets left over that he can hopefully sell to someone else. Once everything is set up, the costs incurred by the printer are the sheets of paper (much of which he has already purchased) and the actual running of the press.

Economies of scale occur when a salesperson has to fly to a distant town to visit a client. Since the airfare will be incurred regardless of how many clients are visited, it seems worthwhile to try to schedule other clients or potential new ones during that same visit. In the same manner as the incremental cost per 1,000 copies of letterhead was brought down, the incremental cost per visit to client or potential client is reduced.

You might say "Well, I've done that!" Well, you've been practicing economies of scale. Very good.

DIMINISHING RETURNS

This region of diminishing returns is analogous to a reversal of economies of scale. That is, there is a point beyond which you have to incur extra cost which means expending some additional effort in order to keep the system in line. Let's say that in the case of the printing press and the letterhead, that because of the nature of the press, it has to be re-registered, or, shut down and re-adjusted after every 10,000 copies. If this is not done, then the letters on the letterhead are not printed exactly where they should be and the result is inferior quality. Assuming that is the case with this particular press, if a customer orders 20,000 copies after the first 10,000 copies, the press must be re-adjusted which is an additional

Table 4-8. Printing Letterhead

Number of Copies	($) Total Cost	($) Incremental Cost Per 1000	($) Average Cost Per 1000
1,000	125.00	125.00	125.00
2,000	160.00	35.00	80.00
5,000	250.00	30.00	50.00
10,000	375.00	25.00	37.50

cost in time and money. If this is not done, then inferior quality sheets are produced and, either the customer accepts the product, or, more likely, the printer absorbs the cost of the rejected material. This is an example of diminishing returns. Although economies of scale were in effect up to the point of 10,000 copies, continuing beyond that without any adjustment resulted in diminishing returns as exhibited by an inferior product.

Another example of this is when you are reading or studying something. During your first hour of reading, you may absorb much material. During your second hour, you may absorb almost as much. Then, when staying up late and really "burning the midnight oil," you find that during your fifth or sixth hour you are really not learning any more than you would in 5 or 10 minutes of the first hour. You are now in the area of diminishing returns and it's best to get some rest and then start over.

UNDERSTANDING FINANCIAL STATEMENTS

The key financial statements are THE INCOME STATEMENT and THE BALANCE SHEET.

The income statement lists the sales, costs and expenses involved in getting these sales, how much was paid in interest for loans or bonds and the taxes that were paid. It does present these in a particular way, however, as is illustrated in Table 4-9.

Here, briefly, is the essence of any income statement. *You take your sales figure and subtract the costs and expenses associated with obtaining those sales. The amount that you now have is called your net operating income, or earnings before interest and taxes.* This figure for earnings before interest and taxes is abbreviated EBIT. The reason it is called this is obvious. It is the numerical value of your net earnings before you have

Table 4-9. The Falcon Company Income Statement (figures in thousands of dollars) for year ending December 31, 1993.

Sales	3,200
Costs and Expenses	
Labor and Materials	2,200
Depreciation	100
Selling	25
General and Administrative	40
Mortgage	50
	2,415
Net Operating Income, or, Earnings Before Interest and Taxes (EBIT)	785
Less Interest Expense:	
Interest on Mortgage	35
Earnings Before Taxes	750
Federal and State Taxes (at 40%)	300
Net Income	450

subtracted your interest payments and taxes. Next, you subtract your interest expenses from this and get earnings before taxes. Then, you calculate and subtract your taxes from this and get the earnings which are your real net earnings, also called net income. This figure represents what you made as real profit during the time period covered by the income statement. Net income is what you are trying to maximize.

There are a few more things about an income statement that you should know

- An income statement covers a definite period of time. This is usually a year, but at times can be a quarter of a year or a month or whatever you want it to be. The period of time that is covered is specified in the title of the income statement as you see for the Falcon Company in Table 4-9.
- When you begin dealing in numbers for the larger corporations, the figures will usually be presented in thousands of dollars and that will be mentioned in the heading of the income statement. This means, that if you have a figure of 1,000, this is really 1,000 × 1,000 or 1,000,000.

Table 4-10. The Falcon Company Balance Sheet (figures in thousands of dollars) December 31, 1993

Assets		Liabilities and Equity	
Cash	50	Accounts Payable	50
Accounts Receivable	300	Accrued Wages	12
Inventories	250	Accrued Taxes	70
Total Current Assets	600	Total Current Liabilities	132
Plant and Equipment	1,600	Mortgage	900
Less Depreciation	400	Total Long Term Debt	900
Net Plant and Equipment	1,200		
		Total Liabilities	1,032
Total Assets	1,800		
		Equity	768
		Total Liabilities and Equity	1,800

- The income statement is also known as a profit and loss statement and because of this is sometimes called the P and L sheet. The income statement can be called an income statement, a profit and loss sheet, a P and L sheet, a P and L, a P and L report-it's all the same thing.

Most income statements will be larger than the one presented here as an example. That's because you will have stock issues and bond issues and many other subcategories. But the example is the essence of an income statement. If you know this, you can figure out the more complex ones.

The next major statement is the balance sheet, an example of which is shown in Table 4-10. The balance sheet consists of three major categories. The first category is the assets of the company. The next is the liabilities of the company. The third category is the equity or net worth of the company which is the difference between the assets and liabilities.

In fact, the balance sheet equation is, considered by accountants, to be as follows:

$$Assets = Liabilities + Equity$$

This is fine if you are an accountant because you list things that way. However, many financial managers, and other people like marketing directors, research and development directors (yes, they also read financial reports) prefer the equation to be written in this manner:

$$Assets - Liabilities = Equity$$

Remember, shifting something from one side of an equation to the other side simply changes the sign of that, so, when we moved liabilities from the right side to the left, we put a minus in front of it. When you stop to think about what that really means, it makes very good sense. This is sometimes written just by the capital letters:

$$A - L = E$$

The same thing applies to you on a personal basis. You have a house, but maybe that house isn't completely paid for. You have a car, and maybe that car isn't exactly paid for. You have a boat, and maybe that is completely paid for. In order to determine your own net worth, you take all your assets like the market values of the house, the car, and the boat, and you subtract from the total what you owe, such as the mortgage on the house and the payments on the car. Then, the remainder is your net worth. You simply take all your assets, subtract from them what you owe, and the difference is what you really have. That's what the balance sheet is for a company.

One of the big differences between an income statement and a balance sheet is that while the income statement covers a definite period of time during which the income was obtained, the balance sheet is, in essence, a photograph of your company at a moment in time. Therefore, there will be a date on a balance sheet showing the date of the "photograph." You will not see on a balance sheet "...for the time period ending...".

Some points of interest about a balance sheet that are worth remembering are:

- The firm's assets are shown on the left side and the liabilities are shown on the right side (usually).
- The assets are listed in the order of their liquidity. Liquidity refers to the ease with which an asset can be converted to cash. Of course, cash is cash so it is the most liquid and will appear first. Plant and equipment may be very valuable but are not very liquid in the sense that they can't

be readily converted to cash and therefore, they're down near the bottom of the asset list.

- The liabilities are listed in the order in which they will be paid off in the event of a liquidation of the company. In the cases where there are stockholders (not in our example), the stockholders' equity which represents ownership, is listed as a liability and will be near the bottom of the list. Usually, if a company is in bad enough trouble that it has to liquidate, there will not be enough left for the stockholders in the first place or they would not be in trouble.

An important point about the balance sheet equation. *It will always balance!* Mathematically, it has to always balance. That doesn't mean you will always like the way it balances. For example, if you have 3,000,000 in assets and 4,000,000 in liabilities you have an equity or net worth of minus 1,000,000. That's not good! It does balance, however. If you have assets of 3,000,000 and liabilities of 1,000,000 you have an equity or net worth of plus 2,000,000. That's good! And, of course, it balances. The balance sheet equation always balances. You want it to balance such that it gives you a good figure.

In the case of the shareholders' (stockholders') equity on the balance sheet, that will be listed as a liability because it is a liability of the company itself to the shareholders.

In the case of the income statement, when net income is arrived at, that net income can be either "retained" as retained earnings which is really "plowed back into" the company, or, it can be distributed as dividends to the shareholders, or it can be split between those two areas. The usual case is to split the net income somehow between those two entities. Retained earnings is a misnomer. They are not really retained like cash or a check sitting in a drawer. But they are put back into the company, i.e., reinvested into the company. The dividends, of course, are part of the return that shareholders usually expect to get, and they come from the net income. This distribution of dividends from the net income is what is meant by "double taxation." It means that the shareholders are taxed twice. Since a shareholder owns part of the company and the company has already paid taxes before dividends were distributed, the shareholder as part owner of the company has already had taxes given to the government from his company. Now, after taxes have been paid and the net income is calculated, a portion of that net income is given to the shareholder as a dividend, which the shareholder must claim as income on his personal tax statement and again pay a tax on it. This is what is referred to as double taxation. In reality, you are taxed two and three times on many things in life. When you go to the theater, you pay for your tickets with income that has already been taxed and you pay an amusement tax to the city on that. When you buy gasoline for your car with your income that is net income, you pay a gasoline tax. And so on and so on with many other things you purchase. When you hear about the principle of double taxation in the world of finance, it refers to the tax on the dividends that shareholders receive.

RATIO ANALYSIS

Ratios tell more than absolute figures.

There are five categories of ratios. They are:

• Liquidity
• Asset Management
• Debt Management
• Profitability
• Market Value

Let's now look at the *Liquidity Ratios*. The first of these is the current ratio.

$$\text{Current Ratio} = \frac{\text{Current Assets}}{\text{Current Liabilities}}$$

See how it got it's name? Current. Using our example of the Falcon Company and referring to the balance sheet, we see that the current ratio for the Falcon Company is:

$$\frac{600}{132} = 4.5$$

Is that good or is that not good? Well, you have to compare your company to other companies in the same industry. Don't compare an airline to a string of movie theaters or to the banking industry or anything like that. You have to compare your company to your own industry.

Where do you get these figures? These figures are available in pamphlet form from companies like Standard and Poor and are available in reference books in the library.

The quick or acid test ratio is:

$$\frac{\text{Current Assets} - \text{Inventories}}{\text{Current Liabilities}}$$

Think about this. What this is saying is: do not count your inventory as a current asset. Take your current assets as listed on the balance sheet and subtract your inventories from them, (i.e., don't count them) and then divide that figure by the current liabilities. An interesting note here is that if you have any inventory at all, this ratio will be smaller than the one we just finished discussing because you are subtracting from the numerator. Therefore, the numerator is smaller, but you have the same denominator, (current liabilities). Therefore, your ratio will be a smaller number. Again, as with all of these, you compare ratios in your own industry.

The next major category is *Asset Management.* You probably have noticed by now that these are appropriately named. These ratios measure how well you manage your assets. The first is inventory turnover which equals sales divided by inventory. If you take your annual sales and divide it by the average inventory on hand you will find a ratio that equals the number of times that your inventory "turned over" during the course of the year.

Generally speaking, the smaller your profit margin, the larger the number of turnover times you'll need for your company. For example, a large supermarket works on a profit margin of 1–3%. This is not much. However, they turn their stock over several times every month (an average figure is used because each item will have a different ratio). On the other hand, the jewelry store which has a profit of at least 100% on all the items in it may not turn over its stock once in a complete year. The jewelry store can "tolerate" a low turnover ratio because the profit margin is so great on the individual items.

The next asset management ratio is total assets turnover which is sales divided by total assets. Take your annual sales, divide them by the total assets and you will obtain a ratio that needs to be compared to others in your industry in order to see how well you are doing.

Debt Management Ratios. The key ratio to remember here is "debt to total assets." This ratio, total debt to total assets, is a good indication of the percentage of debt that your company has incurred or "is carrying."

While it is a ratio, and therefore is a pure number, with no units, it is usually expressed as a percentage. For example, if your debt was $5,000,000 and your total assets were $10,000,000 you would have a debt ratio of 0.50. Usually, people will refer to this as 50% debt ratio. You may hear it either way.

Profitability Ratios are also very appropriately named. They are a measure of your profitability. There are various profitability ratios. Each of them will relate the net income available to common stockholders to something else and, in each case, a ratio will be obtained. Remember, on the income statement (which is the profit and loss sheet) the net operating income, which is earnings before interest and taxes, EBIT, was obtained. Then the interest expense was subtracted from it to furnish earnings before taxes. Then, the taxes were subtracted from that to get the net income. This is—in the case of a corporation that has issued common stock and therefore has common stockholders—the net income available to common stockholders. Even though the company will usually split this income, giving some to the common stockholders, usually in the form of dividends, and "retaining" some in the business, i.e., putting it back into the business or reinvesting it into the business, the entire sum before division into those parts is called net income available to common shareholders or stockholders.

We have then, the ratio called profit margin on sales which is:

$$\frac{\text{Net Income Available to Common Stockholders}}{\text{Sales}}$$

This is pretty much self explanatory. It is, in fact, the definition of profit margin for a company. Certainly, it can readily be seen that the profit margin on sales is a good indication of the profitability of the company.

The next profitability ratio is return on total assets (ROA). This equals:

$$\frac{\text{Net Income Available to Common Stockholders}}{\text{Total Assets}}$$

Here again, we have an equation that is self explanatory. It answers the question, "How much money did we make in relation to the assets we have had to use?"

The last profitability ratio that will be covered here is return on common equity (ROE). This is:

$$\frac{\text{Net Income Available to Common Stockholders}}{\text{Common Equity}}$$

Go to the balance sheet and take your total assets, then subtract from them your total current liabilities, your bonds and the value of your preferred stock, and you will obtain the total common equity which consists of the retained earnings plus the value of the common stock.

The last category is *Market Value*. The most important ratio here is the price/earnings (PE) ratio which is the price per share of common stock divided by earnings per share of common stock. The price per share of common stock is what is being paid for a share in the market. The earnings per share (EPS) value is the net income of the firm divided by the number of shares of common stock outstanding.

This price/earnings ratio is used in the stock market when considering the value of the stock. It makes sense since this category is the market value category.

The five general categories of ratios described above, when used in comparison with your own industry, will give you a good picture of the status of your company. Other categories can be created by you for your personal needs using one value in relation to another. This will give you an indication of the health of your company. If it is a new ratio that you just thought up and you are not sure that it is common for your industry, then compute it yourself for your competitor. How do you do that? Get copies of their annual reports, look in them, extract the numbers that you need, and compute them.

In any case, obtaining copies of your competitors' annual reports is a very smart thing to do. Then you really know how well your competition is doing, and how well you're doing in relation to them.

CAPITAL BUDGETING

Capital budgeting involves the budgeting for, and the computation of, the returns from capital projects. What's a capital project? It's a project that involves an expenditure for a capital item. What's a capital item? That's a large item that costs a lot of money. It can be a big machine of some sort for your manufacturing facility, say, a machine that costs $500,000. It can be the addition of several new vehicles to your sales department's fleet of cars. It can be a major research project for your

Table 4-11.Payback Period

Year	Cash Flow	Cumulative Cash Flow
0	(5,000)	(5,000)
1	2,000	(3,000)
2	2,000	(1,000)
3	3,000	2,000
4	3,000	5,000
5	4,000	9,000

R & D department. It can be the construction of a new building. That's what a capital budget item is.

You select the projects that are the most necessary which, in turn, will give you the most return on your investment. Suppose you had two projects, A and B, and, they were *mutually exclusive,* that is, you could not select both of them—whichever one you select is the one you go with and you cannot carry out the other. This occurs to you in life every day. Suppose you want to go to the ball game and the theater but the events are scheduled at the same time ten miles apart. You have to pick one or the other. They are mutually exclusive projects. There are three common methods for determining the return on projects. You use the one you prefer. Then you can determine which of the projects gives you the greatest return and select it. The three methods are:

• Payback Period
• Net Present Value
• Internal Rate of Return

The payback period method calculates the time required to pay back the original investment. The time is calculated in years. To see how this is done, let's take the illustration in Table 4-11. Initially, you've had an expenditure of $5,000 (This could very easily be $5,000,000 for a reasonably sized company, but here, we'll use small figures for illustration.) So we list for year zero an outward cash flow of $5,000. We do that by putting it in parenthesis. The right column has a cumulative cash flow of minus $5,000 since no money has come in yet. At the end of year one $2,000 has flowed into the company so the $2,000 is listed in the cash flow column for year one. The cumulative cash flow becomes minus $3,000 since we initially spent $5,000 and now have had $2,000 come in to us; the cumulative or net cash flow is minus $3,000. We proceed in a similar fashion for year 2 and year 3. We see that in year 3 we have gone beyond the point at which our cash flows inward have equalled our initial cash flow outward. Assuming that the cash flows were received linearly over the course of the year, we "paid back" our investment one third of the way through year 3. Therefore, our payback period was 2-1/3 years.

Some interesting things to note when using this payback period are as follows:

- It assumes that the money in the cash flow outward was spent all at once.
- It assumes that the cash flows inward occur linearly over the year.
- An advantage is that it is quick and easy to calculate and used to compare various projects.
- A disadvantage is that it does not take into account the time value of money, that is, discounted cash flow analysis.
- A disadvantage is that it does not take into consideration cash flows beyond the payback period.

In some cases those cash flows can be very large, and a project that was not undertaken because it did not have a rapid payback, may, *in the long run,* be the better one.

If the initial cash flow outward is not one large instantaneous cash flow out, but rather a series of cash flows over a period of time, simply include them as negative items as they occur.

When you have two, three or more projects and you are evaluating them on the basis of the payback period method, you would take the one that paid you back the earliest and consider that the "best," and so forth for the second and third place projects. Keep in mind that this only takes into account the time required to pay back the initial investment. It doesn't take into account the overall total profit of the project.

Another method is the *net present value method, NPV.* In this method, the net present values of the cash flows are computed for each year of the projects anticipated or effective existence. A value is obtained. This is done for each of the projects that are possible selections. The one with the greatest net present value is chosen first. The one with the next largest net present value is selected second and so on. (See Table 4-12.)

As an example of a net present value computation, let's take the same project that we did for the payback period example. Glancing back to Table 4-11, you will see the cash flows in the second column and the

Table 4-12. Net Present Value (NPV) at 10% Cost of Capital

$$\text{NPV} = -5{,}000 + \text{PV}(2{,}000)_{1yr} + \text{PV}(2{,}000)_{2yr} +$$

$$+ \text{PV}(3{,}000)_{3yr} + \text{PV}(3{,}000)_{4yr} + \text{PV}(4{,}000)_{5yr}$$

$$\text{NPV} = -5{,}000 + 2{,}000(0.9091) + 2{,}000(0.8264) +$$

$$+ 3{,}000(0.7513) + 3{,}000(0.6830) + 4{,}000(0.6209)$$

$$\text{NPV} = -5{,}000 + 1{,}818.20 + 1{,}652.80 + 2{,}253.90 +$$

$$+ 2{,}049.00 + 2{,}483.60 = 5{,}257.50$$

cumulative cash flow in the right column with the figures in parenthesis indicating negative values and those with no parentheses indicating positive values. Let's assume that the anticipated life of the project is five years.

In year zero, which is the initial time today, an expenditure or cash flow outward of $5,000 occurred. We saw that subsequently $2,000 came in as a positive cash flow in year one, $2,000 in year 2, $3,000 in year 3, $3,000 in year 4, and $4,000 in year 5. Note that we say "came in." Remember, it didn't actually come in yet. We are at a point in time before the actual beginning of the project. We are actually calculating *anticipated* cash flows so that we can determine whether we will or will not take the project. However, when discussing figures of this sort, people often refer to the money as having come in. Be aware that all these calculations are before the fact and all the numbers are anticipated or hoped for numbers. We are establishing the cost of capital, that is the interest we are going to pay on money that we are borrowing for this project, at 10%. In real life, it won't always be an even figure such as this but, for illustration, we select easy numbers so that you are not distracted from the main point of understanding what's going on here. We see NPV as being equal to a negative $5,000 that is represented as the initial cash outflow, and then using Table 4-4, at the end of year one, $2,000 is calculated to its present value, and so on. The other figures are computed in the same fashion and then the entire equation is summed up algebraically. This is shown in Table 4-12 as the original minus $5,000 plus $2,000 times the present value interest factor, 0.9091, for one year at 10%, plus $2,000 times 0.8264, the present value interest factor for two years at 10% and so on. Then, you see, the actual values have been computed and a positive value of $5,257.50 is obtained.

Is it a good number or is it not a good number? Well, you have to look at it two ways. Absolutely speaking, you must look at this and determine if you feel it's a suitable return. Then, relatively speaking, you will compare this to the other values obtained for the other projects that you're considering and rate them according to the greatest return. That's how the net present value method works. It is, exactly as it is named, the net present value.

At this point you may be saying, "How do I know what the return will be 4 or 5 years from now?" Well, you don't really know. You can call what you are doing making a calculated guess, computing, evaluating, or whatever else you want. Keep in mind that this is the financial evaluation of a project. However, you will have research and development information, marketing and sales forecasts, marketing research information, and information from other areas of the company which you will be using in your estimates of the return on investment. You're making the computation here, but you will have information from a lot of other sources so that you will know what is or is not a suitable return.

The third method is *internal rate of return, IRR.* The internal rate of return method is a variation of the net present value method. The internal rate of return, k, is that rate which, when placed in the net present value equation, will make the net present value equal zero. In the case that we have been discussing with the 5 year project and the anticipated cash flows that were discussed in the payback period method, we set up the net present value equation as shown in Table 4-13. Instead of using the 10% cost of capital that we used for the net present value, the net present value is set equal to zero and the rate that causes that equation to be zero is calculated.

How do you solve for k? One way you can do that is by arbitrarily selecting a value (it won't really be arbitrary—you will have a feel for a good value to try) and using it in the net present value equation to see if the net present value comes out equal to zero or not. If the net present value is positive then you will have to select a larger value of k, i.e., a greater rate of return, and try again. If the value obtained is negative, then you have selected a value of k that is too large and you must try again with a smaller value. After a couple of tries, you will zero in on the proper value. You don't have to work out the equation the way it is illustrated in Table 4-13. You can select a particular rate, k, and look up the present value interest factor, PVIF, in the present value interest factor tables such as we did when calculating the net present value above, and solve the

Table 4-13. Internal Rate of Return (IRR)

$$NPV = \frac{-5,000}{(1 + k)^0} + \frac{2,000}{(1 + k)^1} + \frac{2,000}{(1 + k)^2} +$$

$$+ \frac{3,000}{(1 + k)^3} + \frac{3,000}{(1 + k)^4} + \frac{4,000}{(1 + k)^5} =$$

$$= 0$$

Solve for k.

---

equation that way. Alternatively, you will probably have a computer program that does this for you in a couple of seconds.

The point to remember here is that the internal rate of return method is the same equation that is used for net present value, but it has been rearranged. Instead of being given a cost of capital and then solving for the net present value, you set the net present value equal to zero and solve for k, which now is called the rate of return. The evaluation of alternative projects becomes easier because generally speaking you will select the ones with the greatest rate of return.

Should you use the internal rate of return or the net present value since they're essentially the same mathematical equation? That is, pure and simple, your choice of what you feel comfortable using. Actually, whether you select the payback period method, the net present value or the internal rate of return really depends on what you feel comfortable using. The latter two methods take into account the time value of money whereas the payback period does not, but, the payback period is a quick and easy method to compare projects.

Another thing to remember is that during the anticipated life of a project, the expenditures or cash outflows, will not always occur at once at the beginning. They will occur usually in smaller amounts, during year 1 or 2 or further down the line, and these can occur in the same time periods as incoming cash flows. No problem. Simply indicate them in the equations of whatever procedure you select and do the arithmetic. It will work out for you. Just keep track of the cash outflows and when they occur, and the cash inflows and when they occur, and enter them accordingly into the method you choose.

Another method that is used very successfully by some presidents and CEOs is "gut feeling." Many of the people who use the "gut feeling" method are correct as often as those with less experience in business who use the mathematical procedures. Those with significant experience using the "gut feeling" procedure have acquired that wisdom of prediction through their years of experience. Actually, most times when a hunch, or gut feeling, is used in anything—whether it's business or sports or whatever—it's actually a logical derivation that has been arrived at so rapidly that the person is not consciously aware of the steps in the decision making process. So, we won't knock this method. It works for some, and if it doesn't work a large number of times, these people will answer to the board of directors and the stockholders for the wisdom of their decisions.

Another point is that there is nothing wrong with using one method, say payback, for a particular type of project, and another method, say net present value, for another type of project. As long as you use the same method for projects in the same general category, you won't be labelled as being inconsistent.

CASH FLOW

Financial managers are more concerned with cash flows than are accountants. A cash flow system can be thought of as the life blood of the business. What's the difference between cash flows that the financial manager examines and the accountant's ledger book? There are some. Sales may be on credit and therefore a sale is registered in the accountant's books but does not actually represent an immediate cash flow as far as the financial manager is concerned. Some taxes may be listed on the accountant's books for this year but may not actually have to be paid until next year. When they are actually paid represents cash flow. The big item is depreciation. Depreciation is a *non-cash flow expense.* It is a deduction from your income statement but it does not represent cash that flowed into or out of the business. This is usually a large item that represents a major difference between the accounting net profit and the financial manager's cash flow analysis.

The operating cash flows can be larger or smaller than the accounting profits during any given period of time depending on the magnitude of the items mentioned above and the timing of those items.

Financial managers study separate cash flow statements, i.e., separate from the accounting profits. This gives them a feel for how, as the statement says, the cash is actually "flowing" through the business, in both directions.

DEGREE OF OPERATING LEVERAGE

The degree of operating leverage is the relationship of the change in earnings before interest and taxes (EBIT) with regard to the corresponding change in sales:

$$\text{Degree of Operating Leverage (DOL)} = \frac{\%\ \text{change in EBIT}}{\%\ \text{change in Sales}}$$

To illustrate this, let's say that your sales have increased from $200,000 to $250,000 and your EBIT has, during that same sales interval, increased from $60,000 to $80,000. The degree of operating leverage is calculated as follows:

$$\text{DOL} = \frac{\dfrac{80,000 - 60,000}{60,000}}{\dfrac{250,000 - 200,000}{200,000}} = \frac{33\%}{25\%} = 1.32$$

An examination of the equation shows that the higher the degree of operating leverage, the greater the profits will change relative to a change in sales volume. This degree of volatility, so to speak, will occur in the upward or downward direction.

The term leverage is used in another aspect of financial management. A highly leveraged firm is a firm that has borrowed a lot of money in order to operate. If you have a business and you don't owe anybody any money then you are not leveraged. This can be very good. We hear of leveraged buyouts, LBO's. This is simply where some person or group of persons borrowed a lot of money to buy a company out. Generally speaking, the more leveraged the firm is, the more money it has borrowed in some manner or form in order to operate. Here we have calculated a degree of operating leverage. The term leverage is used in an analogous fashion but please don't confuse the two uses of the term.

RISKS AND RATES OF RETURN

Regarding risks and rates of return, much has been said and much has been written. Risks can be visualized by the width of the band defined by the standard deviation in a gaussian distribution pattern. Such a pattern will be found in the statistics chapter of this book. However, at this point, in this chapter, the relationship between risks and rates of return will be discussed very briefly.

Generally speaking, the greater the risk that you take, the greater the loss and/or the greater the return. In business, as in life, if you are conservative, you play things safe, you may achieve small gains or you may incur small losses. This is what being conservative is all about. If on the other hand you are a risk taker, then your decision can result in significant gains or in large losses. Which is it best to be? There is no right or wrong answer to that question. That's a function of your personality and what you feel comfortable doing. A risk adverse person is conservative and likes being that way. A risk taker likes being that way. You have to "do your own thing." If your personality is the same as the personality of the company (this was discussed in Chapter 1), then there's a good match up and a good relationship between you and the company. Do your thing. Know what that thing is regarding risks, and enjoy what you do.

CHAPTER 5

Break Even Analysis

In this chapter we are going to explore break even analysis and look at the following aspects:

- What it is
- Fixed and variable costs
- Assumptions that are made
- An example
- Nonlinear break even analysis

The break even point is that point at which the business neither makes a profit nor incurs a loss—that point at which the total of fixed and variable costs is exactly offset by the revenues. Of course, you want to make a profit, so you always aim beyond the break even point.

For example, as kids, many of us set up lemonade stands. Let's assume our parents bought the wood for the stand, put the stand together, and bought the sign, the pitcher, the glasses, and the lemonade mix. Now, we little entrepreneurs sell 5 glasses at 25¢ and we're very happy to have made a profit of $1.25. The parents know they spent $20 for the supplies and that the initial costs have not been recovered. They realize that 80 glasses must be sold to do so, and there will be no profit until glass number 81 is sold—and even then the entire 25¢ is not a profit. In fact, we need to sell more than 80 glasses to get near the profit because the 80 glasses only covered the initial fixed costs. The revenues from the initial sales contribute in part to recovery of the fixed costs and in part to the variable costs associated with each item, in this case each glass of lemonade.

Break even analysis is that calculation which shows how many units of our product must be sold to cover the initial fixed costs and the variable costs associated with each of those items up to that point. Beyond that point, *which is where we want to be,* each unit sold has a part of the revenue recovering the variable costs associated with it and the other part is profit. This is so because the fixed costs have been recovered at the break even point, and now we are beyond that point, into the realm of PROFIT.

FIXED AND VARIABLE COSTS

We will be discussing fixed costs and variable costs. It is appropriate that we categorize some of these at this time so that you have a good idea of which is which. Some examples of fixed costs are:

- Executive and office salaries
- General office expenses
- Insurance
- Property taxes
- Interest
- Depreciation of plant and equipment

Some examples of variable costs include:

- Costs of goods sold
- Factory labor
- Sales commissions
- Raw materials used
- Direct labor
- Sales expenses

The key points to recognize here are:

- Fixed costs are those which you incur regardless of whether or not you produce and/or sell any item. Take a look at the list. The items on it (and some others you may think of for your own business) are things on which you're spending money regardless of whether you do or do not produce a product. This cost is a single number that is associated with your company and/or your product line. It is not expressed as "per unit" because it is not related to the number of units.
- Variable costs are those costs that are related to the number of units, and therefore are expressed as "per unit." Take a look at the most recognizable one, "raw materials used." It should be obvious from this that the more items that you produce, the more raw materials you have used up,

and therefore the more raw materials you must replace. This is why the variable cost is expressed as per unit. In our discussion that cost will be constant for a large number of units but is considered "variable" in the sense that if you don't make anything you don't incur the cost and on the other hand, if you do make something, you do incur the cost. I mention this here because it sometimes is confusing why you have a constant cost and call it a variable cost. I hope that the reason this is a variable cost is clear now.

- The fundamental break even analysis is based on an assumption that everything manufactured is sold, i.e., nothing has been produced that will not sell or has not been sold.
- We also assume that there are no "price breaks." That is, there is a certain price for which we sell our product on a single unit basis, but if someone buys in large quantities, we then give them a price break or discount. This does occur in real life but is not included in our initial discussion here.
- We also assume (watch this seeming contradiction in terms) that variable costs are constant. In real life, this is not the case because overtime pay, factory labor and bonuses for employees going beyond their rate of production, etc., will change the variable cost. Here again for illustration in the simplest form we assume that variable cost remains constant per unit.

ASSUMPTIONS THAT ARE MADE

Regarding the assumptions that we made above, they are not strong deterrents to obtaining accurate figures. We will use a simplistic example here. When you come across these deviations from ideality, some of which we mentioned above, you simply take them into consideration arithmetically and logically in order to calculate a break even point. We will start with a simple example.

An Example

Let's look at some illustrations first, and then we'll calculate an actual example. Figure 5-1 indicates a simple graph consisting only of straight horizontal line that represents fixed costs. Remembering the definition of fixed costs, you see why we have a straight horizontal line on the graph. Those costs are incurred if we produce zero or if we produce any number

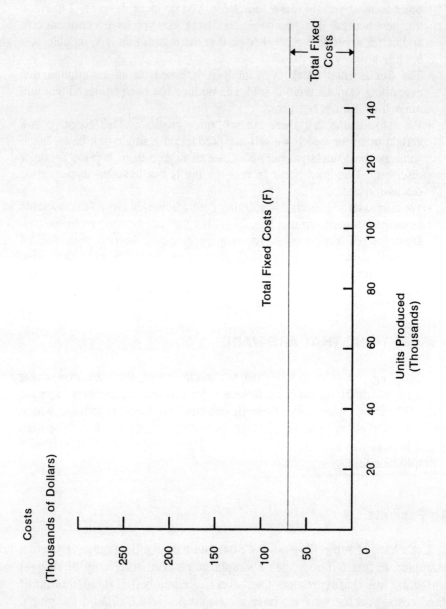

Figure 5-1.

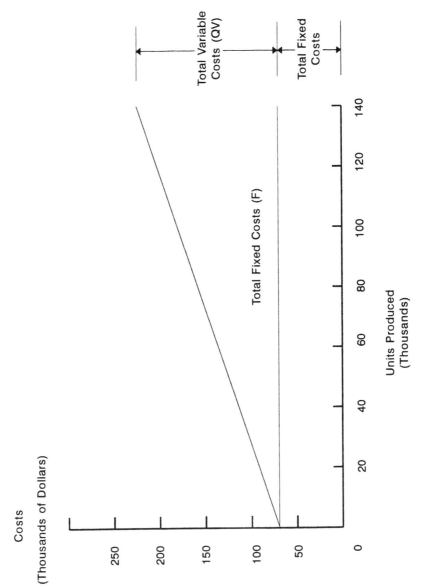

Costs
(Thousands of Dollars)

Total Variable Costs (QV)

Total Fixed Costs

Total Fixed Costs (F)

Units Produced
(Thousands)

Figure 5-2.

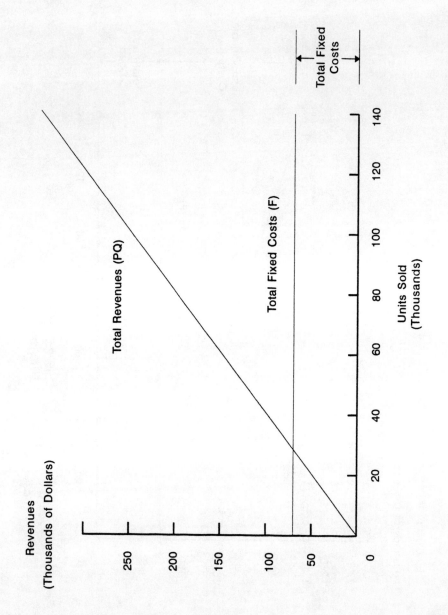

Figure 5-3.

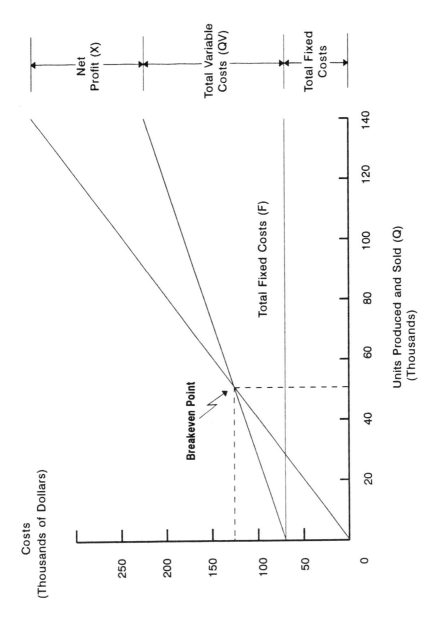

Figure 5-4.

whatsoever of our product. Therefore, we have a straight line on the graph and, it's a horizontal straight line, which means it has zero slope. Next look at Figure 5-2 where we have added the operating costs to this. You see that since there is an operating cost, called a variable cost, per item, we have a line with a positive slope indicating that the more units produced the greater the operating costs. This is, in effect, our variable cost plot. Instead of starting it at the origin of the graph, we start it where the fixed costs line intersects the vertical axis. Remember the fixed costs have been incurred before we ever produced any item. Therefore, the variable cost curve literally sits on top of the fixed curve because, as you have guessed by now, the fixed costs plus the variable costs equals the total costs. By plotting the variable cost "curve" on top of the fixed cost line, that variable cost line automatically represents the total cost.

Now, using the vertical axis as dollars to indicate both costs and revenues, we will plot our revenues. Let's look first at Figure 5-3 where we have plotted the revenues. Essentially, this is a graphical representation of your sales. If you sell one unit at $1, you plot $1. If you sell 3 units at $1 each, you plot $3 and so on and so forth. Therefore, you will have a straight line with a positive slope emanating from the actual origin of the graph.

Now we look at Figure 5-4 and we have superimposed the revenue line with our cost lines, and, as you might expect, the point of intersection is the break even point, and beyond that is the realm of profit.

As an example, we will now refer to Table 5-1. At the break even point, the sales revenue equals the costs. These costs are the sum of the fixed costs and the variable costs. Said more simply, at the break even point, the sales equal the costs. We see that the sales are equal to the price per unit, i.e., the selling price times the quantity sold. That is equal to the fixed cost plus the variable cost times the quantity produced (which we are assuming is the quantity sold). Remembering that when we move something from one side of an equation to the other side, we simply change its sign. We take the mathematical quantity "Variable Cost × Quantity Sold" and move it from the right side to the left side of the equation. We do that for a purpose and that purpose is to get the quantity, Q, in a position where we can factor it out. You see, we actually did factor it out in the next step. Now, we have the quantity sold, Q, times the mathematical quantity price minus variable cost as being equal to the fixed cost. This is not ready to be solved yet. We have to do a little more rearranging. Remember that when you divide one side of the equation by anything, as long as you divide the other side of the equation by the same anything, you

Table 5-1. Break even point. The Sales Revenue Equals Costs.

Let: BE = Break even point, volume, dollars
S = Sales in dollars
Q = Quantity produced and sold
VC = Variable cost per unit
FC = Fixed cost
P = Price per unit

$$\text{Sales} = \text{Costs}$$

$$P \times Q = FC + (VC \times Q)$$

$$P \times Q - (VC \times Q) = FC \qquad (5\text{-}1)$$

$$Q \times (P - VC) = FC$$

$$Q = \frac{FC}{(P - VC)}$$

Now, using numbers,

$$\text{if: Fixed costs} = \$70,000$$

$$\text{Selling price} = \$3.00$$

$$\text{Variable costs} = \$1.25$$

$$\text{then: } 3.00 \times Q = 70,000 + (1.25 \times Q)$$

$$3.00 \times Q - (1.25 \times Q) = 70,000$$

$$1.75Q = 70,000$$

$$Q = \frac{70,000}{1.75} = 40,000$$

will not change the values represented in the equation. Therefore, we can "clear the left side" by dividing that side by the arithmetic quantity (P - VC) but we must divide the right side by that same thing. Then our equation is rearranged so that the quantity to sell to break even is equal to the fixed cost divided by the arithmetic value, "price minus variable cost." Since we said that we are making a calculation at the break even point where sales equal costs, this equation that we derived is the equation for the quantity that must be sold to reach the break even point.

This is not as cumbersome as it may seem. Remember, you know your fixed cost, you know your selling price, and you know your variable cost. You know all the figures involved before you ever produce anything, so therefore, you can make this calculation early on in your manufacturing and selling predictions. Repeating, Equation 5-1 is the equation for the quantity that must be produced and sold in order to break even.

How many dollars in revenue must you make in order to break even? That's easy. Just take the quantity sold and multiply it by the selling price.

Now let's use some numbers in our example. Look at a scenario where our fixed cost equals $70,000 and the selling price of our widget is $3. Our variable costs are $1.25 per item. Then we see that using Equation 5-1, we find that the break even quantity is 40,000 units. That is, 40,000 units must be sold in order to break even if we are going to bring this product or this "run of product" to market successfully. In fact, we shouldn't even say successfully because to be successful we have to sell many more than this in order to make a profit. So you see, the first 40,000 items sold gets us out of the loss range and takes us up to the break even point. The 40,001st item is sold for $3, and, $1.25 of that covers the variable cost on that item, but now, since we have taken care of our fixed cost, we realize $1.75 profit.

Another way of looking at this (but I believe a more simplistic way) is to say to ourselves that we have a $70,000 fixed cost. We have $1.25 variable cost associated with each widget therefore, we will "make" $1.75 on each widget that we sell, but, we have to first recoup or recover the fixed cost. So, now, simplistically, we say to ourselves "how many $1.75s are there in $70,000?" What we do is divide the 70,000 by the $1.75 and sure enough, we come out with 40,000 units. Then, we remember that on each one that we sell we earn $1.75. Now you say that you're in business not just to break even but to make a profit. Of course you are. How do we calculate the number of units that we have to sell in order to make a particular profit? Refer now to Table 5-2. You use the fundamental break even equation. Now however, the Q that you desire is the quantity required to make a particular profit instead of the quantity needed to simply break even, so, you put your desired profit on the right hand side of the equation. You will have to sell more units than required to break even, so now, when you calculate the Q, which we will call Q_p, where the p indicates profit, it

Table 5-2. Profit beyond break even. To calculate the number of units to be sold to earn a particular amount of profit, add the desired profit, P, to the right side of the equation.

Suppose you desire a $50,000 profit. Now:

$3.00 \times Q_p = 70,000 + (1.25 \times Q_p) + 50,000$

$(3.00 \times Q_p) - (1.25 \times Q_p) = 70,000 + 50,000$

$\$1.75 \times Q_p = 120,000$

$$Q_p = \frac{\$120,000}{\$1.75} = 68,571 \text{ units}$$

Dollar Sales $= Q_p \times$ Price $= Q_p \times 3.00 = \$3.00 \times 68,571 = \$205,713$

is equal to the number of units that have to be sold in order to make the profit that you have listed on the right hand side of the equation. Let's say that you desire a profit of $50,000. Then, add that to the right side of the equation as you see in Table 5-2. When you calculate it, you see that you have to sell 68,571 units in order to earn $50,000. In the real world, you will probably round this off to 68,000 or 69,000 or something like that but the mathematical calculation shows the exact number of units required.

What sales revenue is required to get that? Take the number of units and multiply it by the price. That is 68,571 times $3 which equals $205,713. Here again you may round this off to 206,000 or 210,000 but mathematically, the exact number is calculated.

As a manager, you are called upon to make decisions involving investments in equipment utilized to produce an item. These investments involve your fixed costs. Remember the list that contains certain items that fall in the category of fixed costs. Generally speaking, what will motivate you to spend the money to increase your fixed cost? The answer to this is *you will spend money to increase your fixed cost when so doing will reduce your variable cost*. Think about it. Why should you make a large expenditure if you are not going to gain anything anywhere else by it? You might say "Well, I am replacing some antiquated equipment." In replacing that antiquated equipment, you should be reducing your variable cost. You are not just replacing old equipment. In so doing, you are reducing expenditures elsewhere and that elsewhere is in the realm of variable costs. Usually that is. Almost invariably.

Let's take a look at our example and compare it to a smaller investment in fixed costs and to a higher investment in fixed costs. Here, we emphasize, *the fixed costs and variable costs were made up for illustration. The exact change in variable cost as a result of an investment in fixed cost must be calculated by you for your item and your company with all the specifics inherent today.* The numbers selected here are general numbers to illustrate a point, that point being that when you increase fixed costs you should be reducing variable costs, and visa versa.

Refer now to Table 5-3. In that table, the Ex simply refers to the example that we have been using, the L refers to lower fixed costs, and the H refers to higher fixed costs. We see the fixed cost, the variable cost, and the selling price listed. The selling price of course remains the same. We have calculated the number of units to break even and then multiplied those units by the $3 selling price to get the sales revenue required to reach the break even point. And you see that in the case where we have reduced the fixed cost, we reached the break even point sooner, and in the case where we have higher fixed costs, we reached the break even point later. Is this a contradiction to what we just said above? No, it definitely is not a contradiction. Remember, we are not aiming at the break even point, we are aiming at a profit that is far beyond that break even point. Therefore, when you look at a variable cost per item we see that in the case of higher fixed costs, the variable costs have been reduced to $1.00 giving us a $2.00 per item profit and therefore, the profit margin is greater beyond the break even point. This is an important thing to remember. *When you increase your fixed cost, you should reduce your variable cost. You have a greater distance to go to reach your break even point, but, beyond that break even point you have a greater profit per item throughout your profit range.* This is why you calculate the entire market for your products, that is, the total amount you anticipate selling in a particular amount of time, and then you can determine what level of fixed cost investment you will have.

NONLINEAR BREAK EVEN ANALYSIS

An important consideration in discussing a break even analysis is that while everything discussed here is very simplistic such as variable costs remaining constant over the entire range of production, this is not always the case in real life. Your variable costs will change when you start paying

Table 5-3. Changing Fixed and Variable Costs.

	L	Ex	H
Fixed Costs	35,000	70,000	100,000
Variable Cost	1.60	1.25	1.00
Selling Price	3.00	3.00	3.00
Units	25,000	40,000	50,000
Dollars Revenue	75,000	120,000	100,000

overtime, pay various types of bonuses, give price breaks to your customers, and so on. What happens then? Well, what happens is that you will have a *non-linear* break even chart. At the break even point, you crossed into the realm of profit and, with straight lines, you will never go back into the loss range again. With non-linear break even, you can cross again and each time those lines cross, you go from profit to loss to profit to loss to profit, etc. You won't actually cross as many times as we just mentioned but refer to Figure 5-5 and you will see what this means.

An implication of this is that there will be times when you actually will choose not to make or sell beyond this certain amount. And indeed, in this case you are cutting back your profit, that is, your total profit. What you are electing to do is not put the time and effort toward a decreased *margin*. When you see a non-linear break even chart, you can see where you have a narrow profit margin and you may say "I don't care to put the time and effort in for that small amount of per item profit." Of course, you may choose to go beyond that to a greater profit margin. There are also other considerations such as retaining your customers after you tell them you don't have any more material on hand (especially if you tell them you chose not to make the things they want to buy). So you see, as with many things with business, one area is interrelated to so many others.

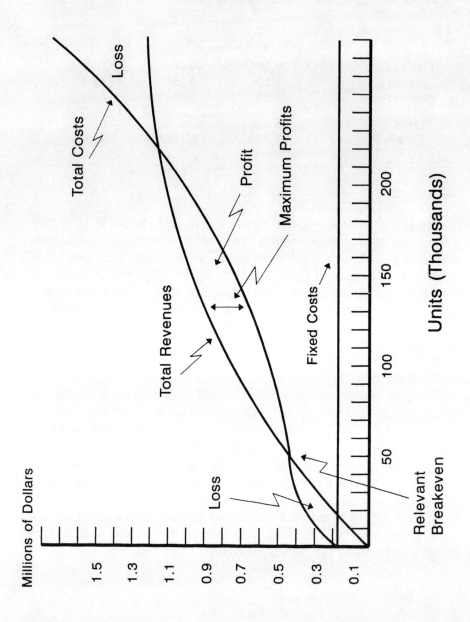

Figure 5-5.

CHAPTER 6

Statistics: A Little Bit, Simply Explained

What managers need in order to make the proper decisions (separate from the common sense and nerve required to make decisions) is *information*. Today, many managers feel they need much more information than they are receiving. Once in a while, this is true. Some extra information over and above what is available is needed for the proper business decision to be made.

In many cases in today's society, the problem is not too little information, but so much available information that the manager is overwhelmed. Most managers will not say that they are overwhelmed. They simply say that they have a lot of data to sort out. The fact is, however, that today, with Management Information Service (MIS) sections in businesses providing so much information, there is an overabundance of it. It's common practice today to see piles of computer printouts on a person's desk. The successful manager is the person who knows what data to extract from the reams of data in that pile.

When you look at multitudes of computer printouts as a smorgasbord dinner, you can find a good comparison. At a smorgasbord, you don't eat everything you see: you simply take that combination of food and beverage that suits your needs at the moment. If you walk down a smorgasbord line you may choose a roast beef sandwich, a little salad, and perhaps a diet soda. Someone else will select what is most suitable for them. The person who tries to select everything, either not knowing what to select or being a glutton for all that is available, usually is seen as a bulky person who stands out as someone who doesn't seem to know what is best for himself.

The same is true with information in business. When you can select that combination of information that is best for your needs at that moment, you are working most efficiently. There may be information in your piles of papers that can be used by other people. Then, shuffle that information to them for their use. So you see, having the necessary information is far more efficient than having an abundance of information that is not sorted properly. It has been said that "Statistics are like a bikini. What they reveal is interesting—what they conceal is vital."

CAUSE AND EFFECT

In sorting out data, it is important to realize if there is a cause and effect relationship between the data. This is referred to as a causal relationship. This is not to be confused with a casual relationship where X only causes Y to occur once in a while. When X regularly causes Y then it's a causal relationship; X and Y represent cause and effect. Here is an example of how some top managers can be misled.

There are various convenience stores throughout the world and in various localities they have their own names. Some are large chains and some are small independent operations. A large chain in the Middle Atlantic section of the United States recently installed sandwich counters where they will prepare sandwiches for take-out, in the belief that this will increase sales.

During my various visits to this store, I observed that the sandwiches are highly customized and therefore take several minutes to prepare. The average sandwich price is about $3. The average regular shopping order is around $7 or $8. A person will come in and buy a milk, orange juice, cheese, etc., and take that to the cashier. Seldom have I seen the two types of shopping occur simultaneously. That is, a person doesn't usually buy a take-out sandwich and walk up and down the aisles and purchase some other things. I noticed that it takes so long to make a sandwich—"What kind of cheese would you like on the sandwich? Do you want red or green peppers? Do you want onions? Do you want mushrooms?" etc.—that several customers who have their arms full of other items and are waiting at the cashier station return the items to the shelves or simply put the items down and walk out because they don't care to wait.

In a discussion with a regional supervisor who reports directly to a vice president of the firm, I asked how the sandwich counter was doing and the reply was that it has boosted sales about 1–1.5% and that this was a very good decision because, for some reason as yet unexplained the regular store sales were down about 3%. Therefore, it is a good thing that they had this good idea of installing this sandwich counter.

The fact is the sandwich counter is *causing* the regular sales to go down. However, a computer printout, or a mountain of data, will not show this. They will give data that reports what the regional supervisor believes. Of course the supervisor believes it because he read the data. If you stand in the store and watch what happens, you will see what is actually going on and see the cause and effect relationship here and then be faced with the decision of either hiring more help or closing down the sandwich counter.

This is an example of where good managers have to get out and *see what's actually going on* instead of only reading data.

Another example is a case where a salesperson for widgets plots the number of customer calls against the volume of sales made. If it is seen that when he doubles his number of sales goals he doubles the sales and therefore doubles his income, we can assume a cause and effect relationship.

Keep in mind whenever you compare data, you must ask yourself if one set of data causes the other set or if the other set is caused by something else.

STANDARD DEVIATION AND A NORMAL CURVE

The curve shown in Figure 6-1 is a normal curve which represents a normal distribution, which is a gaussian curve representing a gaussian distribution which is a bell-shaped curve representing a bell-shaped distribution. This is to say that they are all the same thing. The name gaussian comes from Carl Freidrich Gauss who was a German mathematician/physicist. It is called bell–shaped because it is bell–shaped. It is called normal because we would like to think of it as normal.

Examination of the curve shows that an equal number of values are to the right of the median or average value (in this case) as are to the left, or below the median. More will be said about this type of distribution in a moment. The question does arise as to what kind of distribution you have if it is other than that? A distribution that is different than the normal is called skewed. Figure 6-2 shows a skewed distribution. This figure shows a distribution that is skewed to the left. Others can be skewed to the right, that is, have their predominance to their right side or higher values of the distribution. This type of distribution does not lend itself to the arithmetic that we are discussing here. What is discussed here refers only to a normal distribution.

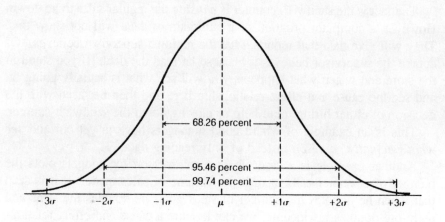

Figure 6-1. The normal curve.

We will define a standard deviation, sigma, σ. Even before showing how to calculate the standard deviation, it is important to know what the standard deviation represents. Referring again to Figure 6-1, we see that we have the center or median line representing the average value of a series of measurements (called "observations"). When we plot the values and see that a normal distribution is obtained, we can then calculate a value called variance, σ^2, from which we take the square root and calculate σ, the standard deviation. What the standard deviation means is that it is the value within which 68.3% of all values for this given set of data will fall. That is, when you calculate your standard deviation and then from the average calculate a range of ± 1 standard deviation, 68.3% of all the values represented by your population (the total number from which your selected number of observations was made) will be within that range. It means that if you made 1,000 observations, then 683 of them would fall in that range. If the population was 1,000,000; 683,000 would be within that range. When you extend the range to 2 σ which is really ± 2 σ, we see that we have now broadened the area under the curve about which we are speaking and we see that a far greater percentage of our population will fall in this new range defined as ± 2 σ. In fact, 95.4% of the total population will have values within that range. You see that ± 3 σ represents 99.7% of the total population.

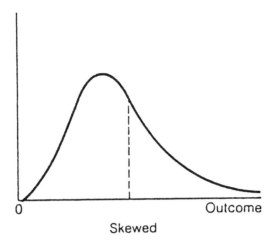

Figure 6-2. Skewed distribution.

This is the very important implication of a standard deviation and a standard deviation range, in predicting the range within which a percentage of the values in a population will exist.

Now, we will do a calculation of the variance (which by the nature of the arithmetic involved is calculated first) and then by taking the square root of that, calculate the standard deviation, σ. For our calculation, we will take a very simplified case. Let's assume that you are manufacturing bottles of a liquid, say shampoo. Let's say that you are packaging 20 ounces of this product. The plastic bottle in which you are packaging it is capable of holding 24 ounces. You have "head space" in the bottle to allow for expansion of the product when subjected to heat such as in the truck during shipment, to allow for a slight "overfill" that may occur, and because you want the bottle to look like it contains more than it does. There are a number of reasons why 20 ounces of material will be packed in a 24 ounces bottle. The important fact here is that while you are trying to get 20 ounces of your product in the bottle, in reality, by the nature of your manufacturing and filling processes, one particular bottle may contain somewhat less than 20 ounces and another bottle may contain more.

We will use another oversimplified example and take only 20 observations here. In reality, if you are filling these bottles at 100/minute which is 6,000/hour, you may be measuring 1 sample/minute. In our case, for illustration in this book, we will take only 20 samples (observations) out of the "population" of many thousand. I emphasize that you would normally take much more than this but the purpose of this is to show how to calculate the standard deviation and therefore we will select only 20 samples. The volume of shampoo will be measured for each bottle of our samples. Our samples will be taken at random time intervals. We will assume a normal distribution. (Actually, 20 samples would not tell you that you have a normal distribution.) In this case, we are assuming that from previous indications of your manufacturing process you know that you have a normal distribution. Measurements that you have made are indicated in Table 6-1. The formula to be used is "the variance = the sum of the squares of the deviations of each sample reading from the average sample reading, divided by 1 less than the number of observations." This is expressed as

$$\text{variance} = \sigma^2 = \frac{\Sigma\ (\Delta^2)}{n - 1} \qquad (6\text{-}1)$$

To get the standard deviation you simply take the square root of the variance. That is why the variance is expressed as σ^2 because when you take the square root of it, you get σ which is the standard deviation. This is expressed as

$$\text{standard deviation} = \sqrt{\sigma^2} = \sigma = \sqrt{\frac{\Sigma\ (\Delta^2)}{n - 1}} \qquad (6\text{-}2)$$

In our case we have rounded to the first decimal for illustration purposes. In reality, you may take this out to any number of decimals that you feel is appropriate for your process. Here, we find that our standard deviation is 0.7. Now we will look at the significance of a "sigma range." Let's talk about the one standard deviation range. This defines a range that is ± one standard deviation from your average. In our case, the average happens to be 20.0. Since our standard deviation obtained from our set of figures is 0.7, the ± one standard deviation range is 20 ± 0.7 which is

Table 6-1.

Observation	Δ	Δ^2
19.8	-0.2	.04
19.6	-0.4	.16
20.1	+0.1	.01
21.0	+1.0	1.0
19.8	-0.2	.04
20.3	+0.3	.09
21.2	+1.2	1.44
21.0	1.0	1.0
19.0	-1.0	1.0
18.8	-1.2	1.44
20.0	0	0
20.0	0	0
19.8	-0.2	.04
19.9	-0.1	.01
19.5	-0.5	.25
20.6	+0.6	.36
20.3	+0.3	.09
19.7	-0.3	.09
18.7	-1.3	1.69
20.8	+0.8	0.64
		9.43
		$= \Sigma \Delta^2$

$$\sigma^2 = \frac{9.43}{(20-1)} = .4963$$

$$\sqrt{\sigma^2} = \sigma = .70$$

19.3–20.7. This is our one standard deviation range which is our average ± one standard deviation. As you see in Figure 6-1, it is indicated that 68.3% of all our data will fall within that range. In fact, in any normal distribution, 68.3% of all the values obtained will fall within the ± one standard deviation range which for our case is 20 ± 0.7 which is 19.3–20.7.

The "two standard deviation range" (or "2 sigma" or "2 σ"), defines the area within which 95.4% of all values will fall and in our case two standard deviations are 2 × 0.7 which equals 1.4 and our "two standard deviation range" is 20 ± 1.4 which is 18.6–21.4.

Similarly, our three standard deviation value is 3 × 0.7 which equals 2.1. Our 3 σ range is ± 2.1 which is 17.9–22.1. This is to say that 99.7% of all the values obtained from our process will fall between 17.9 and 22.1.

Now if any part of our process is changed in any way then our distribution may deviate from normal or have a different average, but as long as everything remains the same we can expect our values to fall within these ranges.

THE STANDARD DEVIATION AND THE WIDTH OF THE DISTRIBUTION

The width of the peak is an important consideration in a normal distribution. We have seen in our distribution that our average was on target to our desired average. In addition, the standard deviation seemed to be reasonably good. Whether you think it was really good or not good at all is incidental to the illustration here. What counts is what suits your process.

Let's look at the cases that can occur. Refer now to Figure 6-3. In Figure 6-3 Project B we see, as the arrow indicates, that the desired average is what we want. However, the distribution, while still being a normal distribution, is very broad. This type of distribution will have a large deviation associated with it. In our case, it looks like it would be equivalent to a standard deviation of 2 or 3 or 4, and that you can readily determine. If it were 4, that would give us a 1 standard deviation range of 20 ± 4 which is 16–24, and that is undesirable. So, the first case that can be encountered is where the average is exactly as was desired or very nearly what was desired but the distribution, while still being a normal distribution, is very broad. This will be evidenced by a high number for the σ or standard deviation.

The next case is illustrated in Figure 6-3 Project A where the distribution is narrow. It is a normal distribution with a good, i.e., small, standard deviation figure, however, imagine that the average is not what we want it to be. For example, using our case, we may have a standard deviation of only 0.2 or 0.3 which would give us the narrow distribution but is different than as shown in the figure. We may want 20 as our target value and we may actually have a peak around 18 which means that we have a tightly

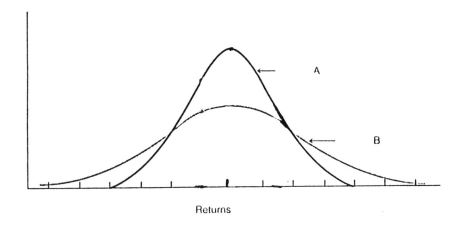

Returns

Figure 6-3. Probability Distributions; A and B.

controlled system but not an accurate system. You can visualize that curve A would be shifted to the left.

"Z" VALUE

There is a value called the "Z" value and some books will show you fancy formulas to calculate it. The "Z" value is a representation of the number of standard deviations away from the mean or average that a given value is. For example, in our case where we had an average of 20 and a standard deviation of 0.7, if we took any isolated value and found that value to be say, one standard deviation away from our average, that is, a value of 19.3 or 20.7, that value is one standard deviation away from our average and therefore it has a value of 1.

Taking another case, suppose we had a value of 18.95. This is 1.05 away from our average. Since our standard deviation is 0.7 and the deviation from the average is 1.05, we take 1.05 and divide it by 0.7 and get 1.5. The "Z" value is therefore 1-1/2 or 1.5.

Why is there such a thing as a "Z" value? The reason for this is that if you are comparing two different, yet similar, systems (say two separate assembly lines in your production area) it is believed better by some people to compare any given value to the mean of that system by computing how many standard deviations that value is away from the mean. Both production lines can have the same average, and they can have somewhat different standard deviations. You don't want them to, but they can, and that may be acceptable to you at a given point in time. Maybe neither production line has given you any indication or belief that it should be shut down to repair the system, but one has a greater deviation associated within it than the other. Taking a given observation or sample from one line and comparing it to a given observation or sample from the other line may show a significant difference if each of them is calculated as a percentage difference from the average. However, when compared by the "Z" value regarding the number of standard deviations from the average, they may be found to be very similar.

For example, if there are two assembly lines and they are both averaging 20, as ours is, but one has a standard deviation of 0.7 and one has a standard deviation of 1.0, a value of 19.3 on the first one represents the same distance away from the average as does 19 from the second line when compared by "Z" values because they are reaching one standard deviation away from the average. Each of them is performing well with respect to "efficiency" of its system. If the comparison was made on a percentage basis, the first value would be 0.7/20 or 3.5% away from the average while the second line sample would be 1/20 or 5% away from the average.

That is the reason for the "Z" value. You may use it or you may choose not to use it. It all depends on how you like to look at your system.

> "Statistics are like bikinis;
> what they reveal is interesting,
> what they conceal is vital."

CHAPTER 7

Graphs, Charts, and Equations

The title of this chapter is "Graphs, Charts, and Equations." But it could justifiably be called miscellaneous arithmetic. The reason for this is that in most cases involving business decisions and numbers of one kind or another, it is arithmetic combined with common sense and judgement that leads to the proper business decisions. This does not mean that there is not a place for advanced mathematics like differential equations and other things such as that; it means that for most of the business situations that you will face you do not need the higher mathematics. Hopefully this is encouraging for you to know because you can now concentrate on the decision making process.

When you need data in order to make a business decision, or a business evaluation of a previous decision, there are certain things that you must ask yourself. They are:

- What am I trying to find out?
- What data do I need?
- How do I get this data?
- Once I get it, what does it mean?
- What is the best way for me to look at this data in order to interpret it properly?
- How should I present this data to others to convince them of my views?

Essentially, most of the data that you evaluate in business involves the scheme presented above, or, some parts of that scheme. There must be occasions when you look at other peoples' presentations of data and you realize that there is a significance there, but you just don't see it. It isn't coming across to you. Most times, it isn't your fault. It's the presenter. When something just doesn't seem right about the data that's presented to you, then take the numerical data and present it to yourself in a different way. Cases in point are when the wrong scales are chosen for the axes of graphs and the dots representing the individual points seem to fall very far away from the line that is drawn to represent the trend illustrated by these points. Sometimes the converse is true; every point seems to have fallen right on the line when in reality you know that that could not be the case with a particular process.

Other cases that you probably have seen involve looking at data on a line chart that could have been better represented on a bar chart. These are the cases where the numbers seem to have some significance to you but the presenter doesn't deliver them in a fashion that is readily understandable by you. How many times have you done this? Hopefully, none of course. However, speaking only of the future, careful attention to *how the data is presented* will insure that you convey your message to your audience, and will further your career.

Think about it. When people can't understand what you are trying to say, how can they evaluate you or your information? When people can understand what you are trying to convey to them, they know your position, realize what you are saying and will listen to you. This does not mean they will always agree with you, but they will listen to you much more than when they can't understand you.

VISUAL MEANS OF PRESENTING DATA

Today, with the aid of computer graphics, there are impressive ways of presenting data. The computer programs available can assist you in conveying the message you want to get across very efficiently. However, don't make the mistake of getting carried away with the computer programs. Know how to use them to present what you want to present. The two classic cases that you must have seen at one time or another are:

• A little bit of data presented numerous ways
• Much data presented so many ways it gets overwhelming

In the former case, the person presenting the little bit of data didn't know how to present it and got carried away with the computer program, or, was so fascinated by what the computer program would do that he forgot the message he was trying to convey. The best way to describe a report like this is *"a lot of style but no substance."*

In the latter case, the presenter was not sure which way would be the best way and therefore presented the information in every way he knew how, thus overwhelming the readers. There is nothing wrong with presenting the data two or three different ways if you have an audience that has various types of people in it (e.g., production, scientists, and sales people) and you want to convey the best to each of these types of people in accordance with what they feel most comfortable reading. This is vastly different than a state of confusion on a presenter's part to the point where the information is presented so many different ways that here again *"a lot of style but no substance."* There is some substance in there somewhere but it got lost in the forest.

The first chart that is used to convey information is a text chart, as illustrated in Figure 7-1. In a text chart, there are certain rules to follow if you want people to read and understand your information. They are:

- Use large print that can be read easily
- Use only a few words. Don't try to get a very detailed message across on one slide or one transparency. You can use more transparencies so why try to get everything across on one? Keep in mind that if it takes three or four or more charts to tell your story, use that many.
- Try to make only a few points. As above, don't try to get too many points of view on one chart. Again, if you try to get one point across on each chart, you can use several charts to illustrate different points.

Keep in mind that before you prepare a text chart or any chart, you have to ask yourself the question *"what am I trying to say?"* Once you can answer this for yourself, you are well on your way to preparing a good chart.

The Line Chart

One of the most common types of charts is the line chart as shown in Figure 7-2. Here we have the horizontal axis called the X axis while the vertical axis is labeled the Y axis. We refer to X as the *independent variable* and the calculated values of Y as the *dependent variable*. For example, if we have the equation $Y = 2X$ and we set the independent variable X equal to 5 then the dependent variable is equal to 2×5 which

Example of Text Chart

Bananas Sold

Month	Tons
January	34
February	43
March	58
April	60
May	52
June	37
July	26
August	22
September	25
October	29
November	30
December	32

Figure 7-1.

is 10. In this case, the value of Y depends on the value of X. Specifically, it is twice the value of X in accordance with the equation $Y = 2X$.

Similarly, if $Y = 4X$ and the independent variable X is given the value of 5, then, the dependent variable Y is equal to 4×5 or 20.

The dependent variable Y "depends on" and is related to, the value of the independent variable X as defined by the particular equation.

Actually, in the line chart, you plot a series of points, each point defined by a pair of values X, Y, then you "regress" which simply means that you draw the line connecting these dots. This is sometimes referred to as "regression analysis." That means that you draw the points and you connect the dots.

A word of caution is appropriate here. If you draw straight lines from dot to dot, you will have what looks to be (and is) a strange graph. It certainly doesn't represent the trend that you are trying to determine. If you have determined the proper number of points, spaced the proper distance apart, you should, realizing the accuracy of your point sets, draw a line that indicates a trend of the point sets and will represent a much neater graphical presentation. Figure 7-2 shows the dot to dot connection. Picture it (or sketch on it with a pencil) "smoothed out."

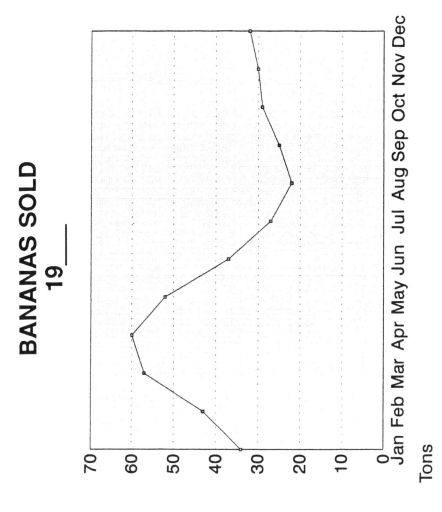

Figure 7-2.

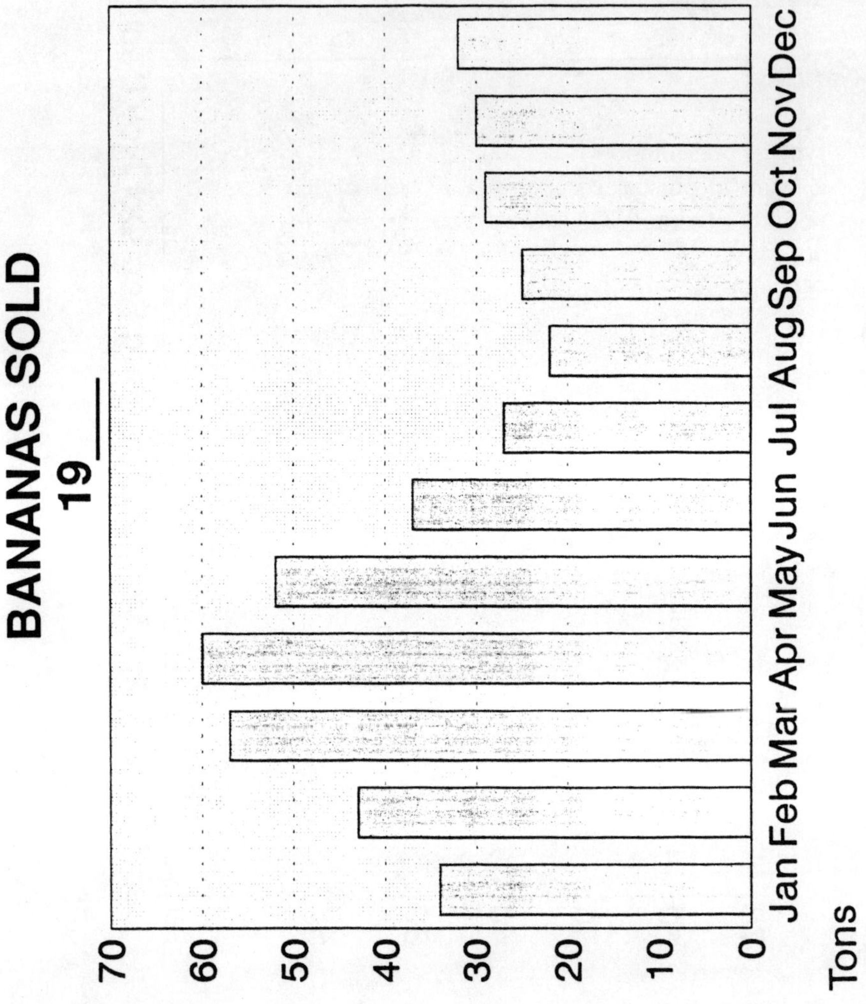
BANANAS SOLD
19__
70
60
50
40
30
20
10
0
Tons
Jan Feb Mar Apr May Jun Jun Jul Aug Sep Oct Nov Dec

Figure 7-3.

If your points are so "way out" that you can't draw a straight line or a smooth curve through them by "rounding" then you may not have any relationship at all to plot. When you do have a relationship between the X values and the Y values, then you will have a reasonable straight line or curve to plot.

The Bar Chart

This type of presentation is shown in Figure 7-3. The bar chart is used when you want to present comparisons of individual accomplishments at distinct periods of time. Of course, you can say that about almost any graph, but let's illustrate the point. A typical example would be presenting sales revenue on the Y, or vertical axis, with the time period of a year, on the X, or horizontal axis. This then provides a pictorial representation of the growth (positive or negative) compared from time frame to time frame.

If this type of data was presented in the normal dot type plot with a curve being drawn, it would still be reasonably readable, but in the bar chart form, the changes are more readily apparent. Rather than dwell on the illustration given here, take some paper, a pen, and a thick felt marker, and sketch a bar chart showing the data that you want to present. Then you will see how well this presents. Actually, if you have a set of thick markers of different colors, you can be very creative with your plot.

There are cumulative bar charts where one bar is place on top of, offset from, or added to another bar at the same position on the X axis. In black and white, this is represented by bars of different shading. In color presentations, this is represented by different colors. For example, you could present the data for sales and the data for profits on the same chart by offsetting the different color bars slightly. Remember that you have a small width across the paper on the X axis instead of only a point, to represent a particular time frame. So you could have a vertical bar representing sales and then immediately adjacent to it, in fact touching it to its right, a bar representing profits. Then when you view this presentation to see performance over a period of time, you can see whether profits did or did not parallel sales.

Another application of a cumulative type bar presentation is to present the sales from different divisions or departments in a company on the same chart.

Table 7-1. Sales by Divisions

Division	Sales in Millions of Dollars	Sales as % of Total
A	100	40
B	70	28
C	30	12
D	<u>50</u>	<u>20</u>
Total	250	100

There is a word of caution here. That is, be careful not to put too much information on the one chart. It will be a "snow job." It will be counter-productive and you will find that you are turning away your audience, instead of enlightening them.

The Pie Chart

This is illustrated in Figure 7-4. The time that you would prefer to use a pie chart is when you are presenting the data, the individual component of which will be equated to the whole. This is to say that the total of all your data will be considered to be 100%. Then the individual parts can be represented by their respective percentages. This doesn't mean that you have to use percentage figures in your chart. You can use the actual numbers representing your data as we did for our produce store sales in our figures. It simply means that you are comparing individual sections to the entire total.

As a case in point, you can plot the data as is shown in Table 7-1. Here we see that a particular company has four different divisions and we see, for a particular year, the sales from each division. Then, in the last column on the right, we have converted those sales to a percentage of the total sales. You can plot your pie chart with (in this case) its four sections by placing the exact sales figures in the chart, each one representing a wedge of the pie, and then listing at the bottom of the chart that the total is $250,000,000 in sales, or you can list each sales division by its respective

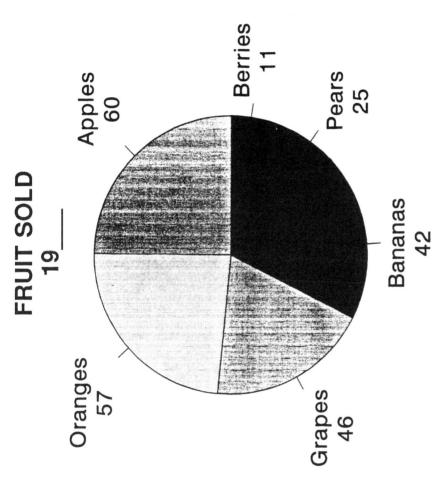

FRUIT SOLD
19___

Apples
60

Berries
11

Pears
25

Bananas
42

Grapes
46

Oranges
57

In Tons

Figure 7-4.

percentage of the 100% total. At the bottom of your pie chart, you can mention that the figures represent percentages of the total sales for that year.

When you want to show a particular division's performance and make it stand out more, you can, in your graphic design, have that wedge of the pie moved out slightly from the pie itself. You can divide the pie the way it is illustrated in Figure 7-4 and then you can pull out slightly the wedge that you want highlighted.

The Combination Chart

You can make presentations by actually combining certain charts. Some will combine more readily than others, both aesthetically, and from the effectiveness point of view, and some won't work very well at all. Experiment with combinations and see which works for you.

For example, you could prepare a bar chart showing sales figures and then you could have a line chart representing the profit from these sales, and superimpose the two. You could, if you wanted, present a separate scale for the Y axis on the right side on the graph and have that offset from the scale on the left and start your profit graph higher than it normally would be. This is to say, that you would, in effect, have two graphs superimposed and that these graphs would have a common X axis but would have different Y axes. This would, however, show a third relationship. The first graph, say a bar chart, would show the relationship of sales to a particular year. The second graph, say a line graph, would show the relationship of profits to those same years. The combined graph would, in addition to showing both of these, illustrate the relationship of sales to profits for each year and over the time span. Sometimes this will be very handy for you, both for your own evaluation and for presentation to others.

SUMMARY

There are various other types of graphs and charts that you could use. One of the typical charts that is in existence today is the organizational chart where you have the solid line connections showing directors reporting to vice presidents who in turn report to the president, etc. Those types of presentations with which you can be innovative have been presented in this chapter.

I must emphasize that in order to select the proper presentation for your data or information, you should first ask yourself "What do I want to say?" Then, when you answer that, you must define to whom you want to say it. This means define your audience. Be aware of their backgrounds and what they do or don't know about the subject matter of your presentation already.

The next thing you want do is sketch the type of presentation you would like to make, using a pen and some wide felt tip markers on a sheet of paper to see how this will look. Many people have lousy presentations because they simply go with one particular type of graph over and over for any kind of data, and they never stop to think of whether it is presenting the data in an understandable fashion. When you take the time to determine which way will best present your data, you will find that your audience will readily understand what you are trying to convey to them. They will be pleased and you will be pleased with your presentations.

CHAPTER 8

Manufacturing

If you are a scientist—and this is especially true if you are a research scientist—you may ask yourself "Why should I care about the manufacturing function?" The answer is thus: as a research scientist, if you design a product that can't be made well from the manufacturing, economic, or marketing point of view, then your company doesn't have a product at all, and your job may cease to exist. That should be sufficient motivation. If you are involved in Quality Control or in Technical Service, it is essential that you know how your product was manufactured so that you can carry out your duties properly.

It is also important to know what type of processes are run in your manufacturing plant so that when you design a new product, you can design it so it can be run on the existing equipment—if that's the directive from management. If, on the other hand, you have the luxury of designing a product and the equipment to be purchased to manufacture that product, then, you enjoy a rare treat.

It is important to keep in mind that some brilliant product development people have designed new products in the laboratory and then these products could not be made economically in production. However, the other side of the coin is that while you are thinking up new products, you shouldn't initially consider the economics because that will put a restriction on your free thinking. If you are a researcher, forget about the economics until you get your initial product (or process) design. Then, as you refine this design and it begins to take shape in your mind, on paper, and up to the prototype state, the economics must be considered. So you see, economics is a very important factor, but for a researcher, not brought in at the very beginning of the creativity process. It is, however, an important consideration soon after that.

Some questions to ask yourself when designing a new product are:

- Can it be made?
- Can it be made economically?
- Can it be made of materials that are readily available?
- Will it sell in the marketplace?
- Can people with certain skills make this?
- Can machines produce this?
- Can a particular quality level be obtained consistently?
- Can we test it consistently for a particular level?
- Will it be satisfactory from a regulatory point of view, i.e., environmentally clean, etc.?
- What other considerations are relevant to your particular product?

TYPES OF PRODUCTION SYSTEMS

There are three types of production systems. They are job-shop, batch or continuous.

Job-Shop

This is where each order is an individual job. Each product is customized for a particular customer and production is scheduled with the necessary parts either being in stock or being ordered for production of the job.

Batch

Here, several items are made at one time using raw materials, each of which has its own characteristic identification, or lot number. Then, this batch, or lot, of final product is set aside for shipping, and a new batch is started.

Continuous

A continuous operation occurs as the name implies. Items are produced continually and the raw materials are replaced as they are used. In this type of operation, more effort is required to keep track of the lots and identification numbers of the raw materials, since as a particular lot of a given raw material is used up, another lot with a new identification number is incorporated into the flow of the system. Additionally, a lot number is assigned to every X number of items that come off the production line. This is done for tracking purposes, both for the consumer and for you, the manufacturer. The size of the lot is arbitrarily selected by you, the manufacturer. In reality, it is not so arbitrary. It is a number that is large enough to accommodate many individual items (sometimes hundreds, thousands or millions depending on the item) yet it is not so large that it is comprised of several lots of component A and several lots of component B, etc., thereby preventing accurate *traceability* of the materials that went into that lot if a problem should arise after the product is in the market-place.

In reality, there are many processes that are combinations of batch and continuous. For example, in tire manufacturing, a batch of compounded rubber formulation is produced and then that batch is used for several tires. The tires are continually produced in the molds one right after the other, each having been molded for several minutes. The batches are produced in rapid succession so you might say "the batches are continually pro-duced." There is nothing wrong with this. That is just the way things are. Some batches are continually produced. You simply realize this and maintain the system that will enable you to have *traceability* of your ingredients.

INPUTS TO THE PRODUCTION PLANNING SYSTEM

When management is planning production of a product there are certain things that must be considered. They are:

• Raw material availability
• Market demand
• Economic conditions
• Knowledge about the competitor
• Legal status
• Current work force
• Inventory levels
• Activities required for production

These inputs may seem obvious to you. Hopefully, they do. But they are mentioned so that you don't forget them.

SOME KEY PERSONNEL

The individual workers on the line are extremely important as are the supervisors and the foremen. Inspectors and shippers play important roles—their positions are self explanatory by their titles. However, there are some positions that are key and are sometimes overlooked by people who are not in production. Most people will agree that the plant manager "runs the plant," and as such is responsible for everything that goes on in it. This obviously is a necessary position. There are two other positions that are extremely important. They are the planner and the scheduler. In some cases, these are one and the same person, i.e., one person does the planning and the scheduling. In other cases, these are two separate people.

There is a narrow line between what could be called production planning and what could be called production scheduling. Generally speaking, the things that are going to be run next week in your plant are the responsibilities of the scheduler. When the time frame extends into what is going to be run more than two or three weeks from now, this becomes the planner's responsibility.

Keeping in mind that these could be two different people or can be the same person performing both functions, depending on the size and nature of the operation, let's just call it all planning, and say a few words about it. The planner must know the production processes, the raw materials that are available, or when those materials will be received, the personnel and the machines that are available and the possible problems that can be encountered. Think about it. How can you plan the production of products if you don't know the product or the system? Therefore, the planner is a very important person. This is why planners many times go on to be plant managers. When a plant manager gets promoted, or retires, the successor often is the person who was the planner because that person is extremely knowledgeable about the entire manufacturing operation.

Why do you care about this if you are a researcher? This is the person who is going to schedule the manufacturing of your product. More importantly, after your new product has made it through the pilot plant stage, and is being scheduled for the first production run, this is the person who plans or schedules it. You want to know this person well because you want your new product scheduled and you want to be notified so that you can watch it being manufactured and catch any potential problems before they become major ones. You want your new product to be a success. You want to see it in its initial production run. You want to know what to expect out of that production run. You and the planner can make a successful "run" if your product is amenable to the system—and it's the planner who can tell you if it is.

Another important consideration for you as the technical person and for the plant manager, the planner, the scheduler, and others in the production area, is that you are familiar with the production process that will be applied to your product with regard to the chronological order of the steps and also, *with regard to the most expensive step, and the next most expensive step, and so on.* Why is this important? It is important because if you seem to have a good product but the economics are not favorable, and you are familiar with the costs of each step in the process, you can direct your activities toward the most costly steps and therefore bring your product to fruition faster. In some cases, it is the difference between bringing your product to fruition or not bringing it there at all.

TOTAL QUALITY MANAGEMENT (TQM)

The concept of Total Quality Management, or TQM as it is commonly called, is really not a new one. It has been around for years. It is new in being called TQM, the name that has made a lot of money for consultants. There are very high fees extracted from company managements that want to have TQM and are not sure in their own minds what it is or when they have it.

In brief, the concept means that there is a quality consciousness and attention everywhere along the production of a product—from the initial design of the product, to the set-up of the system, to the receipt of the raw materials, on through the line, to the final packaging and shipping of the product, and even after the product is in the customer's possession. In the old days, the manufacturing process was reasonably good, was run, and then there were inspectors, who at the end of the production line sorted out the bad. When you wanted to tighten the quality control procedures, you had the inspectors look more stringently at the products and sort more tightly. Here, you "sorted out some good stuff with the bad stuff" but were willing to pay that price so you could increase your quality level. You rejected the materials that were out of specification and, either threw them out or reworked them, depending how far they were out and what your product was.

Nowadays, with the principles of TQM, business tries to "make only good stuff and no bad stuff" in the first place, therefore there is theoretically very little or no undesirable product to be sorted out. The quality concept exists throughout the entire business (not just manufacturing) flow. You still have inspectors, but there are significantly less defects. Since the overall quality is higher, less inspectors are needed, less material is rejected, less material is reworked, etc., and therefore, it costs less to produce the high quality with the TQM concept than with the "sort out the bad ones" principle. Think about it. It seems reasonable that it would be cheaper to make your products right in the first place than to make them at a low quality level and have to do all the sorting out.

Now you know the concept of TQM. Implementing it in your company can be done easily and inexpensively, or you can choose to incur a high consulting fee.

JUST-IN-TIME (JIT) INVENTORY

In a JIT inventory control procedure, the necessary components or materials arrive in the production area "just in time" for assembly into the final product. This precludes large storage costs. Depending on the product you manufacture, the JIT concept can apply to materials coming from your warehouse to the production area when needed or, in the case of some very large items (such as tractors or other earth moving equipment) the materials can arrive from your supplier to your plant just in time for your production assembly.

Let's look first at the inventory costs. There are three different costs:

• Ordering costs
• Carrying costs
• Costs of running out

Your ordering cost is constant per order. Your carrying cost is your cost to store so many parts in your inventory. This will vary with the number of parts you store. If you order "a few parts" frequently, you have a small storage cost but a large ordering cost since you order many times. On the other hand, if you place a few large orders, your ordering costs are minimized but your carrying costs increase because you are carrying a large number of items. So as one goes up, the other goes down. There is a quantity called Economic Order Quantity (EOQ) which calculates the total of these two that represents a minimum cost of ordering. For example, when you calculate so many parts per order and figure how many of those parts you will use in a year, you can calculate the number of orders per year for a particular part. If you calculated ordering fewer parts more frequently, you would come up with different totals. If you calculated ordering larger numbers less frequently, you would come up with different totals. When these are calculated, or plotted out, there is a total that is the lowest of all the totals calculated and this is the EOQ.

The cost of running out is not always taken into consideration, although it can be a very high cost. The cost of running out of an inventory item in a retail store not only leads to the loss of that sale, but when the customer goes to another store to make the purchase of that item, the customer may be swayed over to becoming a regular of that store for other items. Additionally, the customer passes the word on that you were out of a particular item, and so on and so on. The main point here is that you don't just lose that one sale. You may lose a lot more.

If you run out of an inventory part in a production line, you must stop the entire production line. Here is where you walk a tightrope with JIT. You can minimize your inventory costs by having materials arrive either into your plant from the supplier, or at your production line from your warehouse just in time. As long as they arrive just in time, everything is fine. If that occasion arises when they don't arrive in time, your production line will stop, and now you are spending a lot of money to run your plant and you are not producing product.

Here's a handy sign to keep in mind:

```
+---------------------------------+
|                                 |
|            SPEED                |
|                                 |
|           QUALITY               |
|                                 |
|            PRICE                |
|                                 |
|          (Pick any 2)           |
|                                 |
+---------------------------------+
```

Let's take a case in point. You want a supplier to deliver a part or shipment of parts to you exactly when you need them, and not before. You are not the only customer that supplier has. That supplier has to change his schedule to be available for you when you need the parts, which means he has to adapt shipments to his other customers. He is not going to do that free. The JIT concept is good in theory, but don't assume that you are not going to have to pay for this service. It is a good concept and it may work well for you. Just realize that when you first read about it, it is very idealistic. In reality, some serious things can result if things do not go as planned.

OTHER TYPES OF INVENTORY

In closing this section of the inventory portion of manufacturing, it is important to mention the three types of inventory that you have. Please don't confuse these with the three inventory costs. They are different things. The three types of inventory are:

- Raw materials
- Work in process
- Finished goods

When you are running a production line, you have parts in storage waiting to come onto the assembly line, you have work that is in process along that assembly line, and then you have other parts that are made, packaged and waiting to be shipped to the customers. Actually, your accountants want to know these figures so that they can keep a continual track on the assets of the company. From the manufacturing point of view, you want to make sure that the work is flowing through your assembly line. If you consider your assembly line not just as the physical aspect that you see in the plant, but from the raw materials, to the work in process, to the actual shipping of the product point of view, you will have a good perspective on the dynamics of how the plant runs.

CHAPTER 9

Accounting

Why should a technical manager know anything about the accounting function? Put that question with several other questions and the answer may now jump out at you.

- How are you and your department listed in the ledger books?
- Are you listed as overhead? (Especially if you are a research manager)
- Do you feel that you always get your fair share of the budget, or do you feel that you should get more money allotted to your department?
- Do you believe that if you knew more about how the money is coming into an organization and how it is being spent by your organization that you could get more for your department?

As you answer these questions, you can determine whether you do or do not know enough about the accounting function. Maybe you want to learn more.

In Chapter 4, we covered the subject of Finance. We mentioned that the financial manager makes many investment decisions relevant to the growth and existence of the firm. The financial manager gets the information from the accounting manager or vice president or director or whatever you want to call that person. The accounting function keeps track of the inflows and outflows of money through the company.

ACCOUNTING AND BOOKKEEPING

Bookkeeping is the process by which the basic accounting data is systematically recorded. These recorded items are income as revenue from the sale of products, and expenses from the business operations such as the rent, wages, cost of goods sold, and more. The accounting function is the overall function of keeping the financial information readily available for use in making financial decisions. It is the accounting principles that determine which transactions should be recorded in which ledgers, etc. Financial statements are prepared by accountants and given to financial managers for evaluation and financial decision making.

BUDGETS

The budget is determined by the sales forecast. Think about it with regard to your own financial planning. If you are going to want to take an expensive vacation next year, say a three-week around the world tour, you have to forecast a few things about yourself. You will "forecast" your anticipated income next year. Will you get a raise? Will you get a bonus? Will you still have a job? Based on what you believe about your current job existing or expanding, you will estimate your next year's income and then you will determine whether you can incur the expense of the large vacation. You do this for any large item such as the purchase of a new car or sending kids to college. The same thing applies to business. In order to determine what you can spend on those things that you want to do next year, you have to anticipate your income. That income is the profit portion of the sales revenue. Therefore, we say here, again, the sales forecast is the basis for the budget. The accountant keeps track of what is actually happening with regard to cash inflows and outflows. The financial manager determines how cash received by the firm will be invested in order to have more cash received by the firm in the future.

WHAT ACCOUNTING DOES

Accounting provides information on the firm's financial condition to various interested groups. They are:

- The management of the firm
- The company's stockholders and the general public (if it is a public corporation)
- The Internal Revenue Service

Information is given to the general public in the form of the annual report. For large corporations, these are very fancy and cost a lot of money to be printed. The purpose of the annual report is to tell the general public how good the company is doing and to stimulate investment by the general public in the company and "market activity" of the company's stock. When you read an annual report of the company, the letter from the chairman will reflect the philosophy of the company, but even before you read that, turn to the statement of the auditors. The auditor is an independent reviewer, usually an accounting firm that is hired by the company to audit the books and verify that everything is accurate and in accordance with generally accepted accounting principles. If you go first to this portion of the annual report and the auditors say that they have not yet confirmed the accuracy of the data, then don't waste your time reading anything else. If the auditors do say that everything is okay, then you can go to the statement of the chairman of the board, and you will get a reflection on the philosophies of that person and of the company.

Whenever a company has a bad year, and it's due to a foul-up on the part of the president or the chairman, you will usually read something like "Due to international monetary fluctuations and our investment in the such and such international plant..., etc." You will not see a statement to the effect of "I fouled up by making some wrong decisions and I'll try to do better next year." But that is the way life is. You will, however, find accurate accounting data in the financial reports that are listed in the annual report. You will see the trends of the various financial categories such as income, profit, expenses in various categories, and much more. So you see, an annual report will tell you the philosophies of a company, where it's coming from, and, where it's going.

COST ACCOUNTING AND MANAGERIAL ACCOUNTING

Cost accounting determines the cost of manufacturing a particular product or providing a particular service. This can get to be quite complex at times. This is part of managerial accounting which is the function of providing the proper information to the management of the company so they can set up the budgets and review personnel performance.

It is significant to note that the companies must also report to the Securities and Exchange Commission (SEC) which requires its own form of compliance accounting from publicly traded corporations. When a company issues stocks or bonds to be traded on the market, it must follow certain procedures in accordance with SEC regulations. While the annual report contains much information of interest to the general public, the SEC wants to know even more about the backgrounds of the top level managers.

At this point, let's look at some of the costs that the accounting function itemizes. The two major categories are *fixed* and *variable*.

Some examples of fixed costs are:

- Depreciation on plant and equipment
- Rentals
- Salaries of research staff
- Salaries of executive staff
- General office expenses

Some examples of direct or variable costs are:

- Factory labor
- Materials
- Sales commissions

ACCOUNTING SYSTEM PROCEDURES

A good accounting system keeps track of every transaction by maintaining all transactions accurately and honestly in the accounting "books." In some cases, smaller transactions can be grouped together for convenience under the title "petty cash." All large transactions are maintained as separate actions in the accounting books. What is defined as a large transaction depends on the size of the company. Generally, a petty cash transaction consists of only a few dollars. There is no magic number that can be listed here that can separate a petty cash transaction from a large transaction; it will depend on the size of your company and the departments within your company.

The accounting system procedures include the bookkeeping process. In this, a series of things is included. Some are:

- Original documents. These are the documents that record the transactions at the time they are made. These are things such as receiving records, checks, employee time cards, etc.
- Journals. These are the "books of original entry." The transactions are listed in chronological order in the journals. There is always a general journal. There can be several special journals that contain certain types of transactions. There are sales journals, purchasing journals, and cash

journals, which include respectively, sales, purchases, and cash transactions.

THE LEDGER

In order to use the journal information more readily, the items in the journals are individually posted (transferred) to a ledger account. An account is simply a record of an increase or decrease in a type of asset, liability, income, expense, or capital item. A book containing a number of accounts is called a ledger. At this time, let's look at an example. Suppose you are a small business person who buys a particular type of machine used in your production process for cash. (You very well may not normally purchase this for cash. You may purchase this over a time in a series of payments, but for example here let's assume you purchased it with cash.) You have acquired the machine and you have spent cash in order to do this. Therefore, you *credit* the asset account and you *debit* the cash account.

FINANCIAL STATEMENTS

These are the statements that are prepared periodically for informational purposes to the management, the general public, and the regulatory agencies. These include the profit and loss statement, the balance sheet, and others, as described in Chapter 4.

CONCLUSION

Now you know some things about the accounting function. So, what do you have to know as a technical manger? What are you going to do with this knowledge? Well, the main point here is to keep aware of the expenses you incur in running your department. In plain words, know how much it costs to run your department.

Know how the company runs financially and know where your department fits into that scheme. The more effectively you utilize your budget, the larger budget you will get the next time you ask—which is usually the next year.

A word about budgets. Let's use an example here. Let's say that you are walking down the street with your fiance and you ask your fiance, with whom you are deeply in love, to hold your hand. Your fiance says "No, thanks." You begin to wonder, if your fiance loves you, why can't you hold hands while walking down the street. Now extend this analogy to your company. Your company says it loves you. You ask for money in next year's budget. If other departments have budgets that are significantly larger than yours and you feel you are not getting your share, then you have to ask yourself if your company loves you. The amount of money that you get in your budget will not be identical to other departments within the company because some are larger, some are smaller, and they have different functions. However, whether your budget is ample or tight is a measure of how much your company loves you. If other departments have ample budgets with which to work and yours is very tight, then your company or the vice president of your division or whoever, does not think as much of your department as you think he should.

There is another possibility here. The company could be in dire straights and having financial problems. If this is so, then no one will have an ample budget and you all have a big job at hand at getting the company solvent again. Think about it, though. If you are doing good and your company tells you it believes you are doing good, it will give you reasonable funds with which to work because the company knows it takes money to make money.

A reminder just one more time. You don't have to be an accountant, but you should know what the accounting function is and what the difference is between that and the financial management function. You have to, in a matter of speaking, be an accountant and a financial manager for your own department.

PART 2

THE ELEMENTS OF THE TECHNICAL AREA

CHAPTER 10

The Technical Function: Overview

As we consider the technical function, we will use such terms as:

- Technology
- Invention
- Patent
- Innovation
- Research and development

In scientific worlds, terms such as Research and Development are tossed around as glamorously and as loosely as the term Marketing is in the business world. We mentioned earlier in this book that marketing is a glamour term and a glamour area. There are many people in the business function who claim that they do marketing, when in reality they do not. A similar thing is true in a technological area. They claim they do research or development, or research and development, and in fact they do not. On the other hand, there are many people who do not even think a lot about it or even try to categorize it and in fact, they do perform research and technological activities. Here, we will try to show some differentiation between the terms so that at a very minimum, some people can be aware of what they are doing. More importantly, when you budget certain activities, you want to know what those activities really are so that you can determine your Return on Investment (ROI) from that budgeted activity.

Let's look at it from both ends of the spectrum. Let's say that you are a manufacturer of T-shirts with various designs silkscreened onto them. You might even consider that you have this business as a part-time venture, or if you want, you can figure that you have this business as a full-time venture, but at the moment, maybe you are the only employee or you have one other employee. In any case, it is a small business. Suppose you speak with the supplier of the fabrics for your T-shirts and you decide that you want to manufacture some T-shirts out of different fabrics so that they may be more wrinkle free, water resistant, or whatever. You obtain samples from your materials supplier and then you might try washing them and seeing how they dry, or deliberately wrinkle them and see if they keep the wrinkles or if they resist wrinkles. What you are doing is research.

You might ask the supplier of your coloring materials to provide you with swatches of various materials that have different colors on them. Then you may want to see how light or fade resistant these colors are on the fabrics that you just researched. You may want to see how washable these colors are. You may put them in your own washing machine and dryer to see if the colors hold true. This is research.

Then when you have decided on new fabric and new colors and you combine them, you have undergone the development phase of research and development. Actually, if you had asked your existing customers what fabrics and colors they may want in the future, you would have done Market Research.

On the other hand, companies like Exxon and General Motors spend millions of dollars a year on research and development functions and have thousands of people on their research and development staff. The principle is the same. They are doing the same thing you are doing with the T-shirts; they are just spending more money and researching more things.

In the larger companies, research and development may be two separate functions contained in separate buildings. In smaller companies (and sometimes in the larger companies) research and development are functions carried out by the same people.

Additionally, the development part of research and development usually includes a product or a process model to determine the feasibility of this new idea becoming a product.

BASIC RESEARCH

Basic research is a scientific investigation of something usually without knowing the ultimate end use of the knowledge that will be obtained. In today's society, this is not too often the case. There is basic research carried out, but there is some knowledge as to what will be the uses of the information gained from the research. For example, basic research into the nature of light may not have a definite outcome in mind. However, it can be readily speculated that the outcome can be used in communications, energy transfer mechanisms, and more.

APPLIED RESEARCH

Here the research is directed toward identified applications.   For example, when a pharmaceutical company is directing research toward something that will reduce high blood pressure, it has already identified the causes of high blood pressure and is directing this research to overcoming these causes, or circumventing these causes. A vasodilator is a compound that dilates the veins and arteries in the vascular system thereby causing a reduction in blood pressure. That is one mechanism by which such a compound can function. This is one route that a firm can take in reducing high blood pressure.

A tranquilizer that calms a person down and thereby reduces stress in a person and in turn lowers blood pressure is another route to be studied. In these cases, we have applied research. We know the end that we seek and we are directing our research toward achieving the end.

INVENTION

This is a term that has been used and abused. First of all, many persons say that any invention has to be patented. No invention has to be patented. It is good protection for the inventor to patent a process or a product. It is not necessary to do so.

Who would not want to patent an invention? Well, keep in mind that when you patent something, you file in the Patent Office and those records are open for public inspection at any time. While you do have exclusivity for 17 years on the one hand, you have now in essence just revealed your invention to the general public. Some companies, such as those who produce rubber and plastic items elect not to patent their formulations. They do this in the belief that the other factors involved in the production process, such as time, temperature, pressure, etc., are such that no one can duplicate their product without seeing the formula and all the conditions relevant to the manufacture of the product. Therefore, they believe they will have protection for an indefinite period of time simply by not revealing to anyone the formulation and conditions of manufacture.

Most companies, however, prefer to patent a product or a process and reap in all the rewards they can in the 17 years during which they have exclusivity. More about this in the section on patents.

An invention is a device, a technique, or a process that will result in a significant change in a technological application. The application is very important to the invention. There have been many people through the ages that have come up with new ideas that had no immediate application, and hence, there was no invention. You must be creative in order to invent something. When you do invent that something, you must be ready to answer the following questions:

- What is this?
- What does it do?
- Why is it better than what we already have?

Attempts have been made to identify the characteristics of an inventor. The general consensus is that some of the characteristics are:

- Extreme curiosity
- Determination
- Persistence to the Nth level
- Some scientific background
- Creativity (Which is very difficult to define. It seems to be the ability to relate facts that most other people do not see as related and to put these together in such a way as to lead to a conclusion that results in the new idea or invention.)

PATENTS

We already mentioned that you don't have to patent something and we have illustrated above a case where some persons would prefer not to patent something. In most cases, however, it is a good idea to obtain a patent.

In today's society, when a person is working for a major corporation, the patent is assigned to the corporation. The person may get his name on the patent but the patent is *assigned* to the corporation. If the person is in elite status and in the creme de la creme hierarchy of inventors within a company, that person may be in a position to share (profit sharing or percentage basis) in the rewards that are obtained by the company. This is usually not the case. The reasons for this are two-fold. First, many inventions are not the result of one single inventor, but are rather the result of the integrated efforts of various persons and departments within a corporation. Second, the corporation is so much larger than you are and it will prevail.

When talking to friends about an invention that you believe you have, you may hear from one or more of those friends, "Oh, you don't have to get an attorney. You can do the patent search yourself and you can file for the patent yourself for only $300 and save yourself a lot of money." Well, you can do the search yourself and you can file yourself, but it costs a lot more than $300. Generally speaking the fees are as follows:

Search $500-$1000
Patent Applications $2800-$10000
Filing Fee (Government) $340
Drawing $250-$500

If you do your own search and your own patent application, you can save yourself the money that is associated with the first two items. However, the patent examiners have a way of bouncing things back to you and the patent attorneys have a way of resubmitting them and ultimately getting them through. If you are that good, then you can do your own application. The filing fee is a governmental fee. Most attorneys will charge that and not add any increment for themselves. Actually, when you submit that check, whether you do it yourself or whether you do it through your attorney, that check is made out to the Patent Office.

With regard to your friends who are advising you to file on your own, you will do well to avoid them in the future. At a very minimum, ask how many patents they have that have resulted from them pursuing it on their own. Ask them if when a tooth needs drilling and filling, they do that on their own without going to the dentist. Think also that if you really want to make a big bundle of money on your patent, the figures that are cited here are really nominal figures, if your invention is that good and you intend to market it and make a lot of money on it. If your invention is only going to earn $1000 or $2000 for you in the first place, then you don't really have a big market and the whole act of patenting in that case is questionable. (Except, of course, for the ego part of it. There is an ego part—personal satisfaction—in obtaining a patent and this is an important aspect to be considered.) The figures given above are not idle speculation. My patent is pending on my sustained release fertilizer mechanism product. This is to say that the search has been performed and my application has been submitted and is going through the channels of the Patent Office right now. The actual patent should be received any time now. This is my own invention. The actual patent application was made through my patent attorney, Eric La Morte. He is one of the 1% of attorneys that is registered with the Patent Office (one criterion of which is to have an undergraduate degree in a science or engineering field), and his services have been worth every bit that I have spent.

For further reading on patents and how to market ideas on them, I recommend the book *Millions From the Mind* (Alan R. Tripp, Amacom, 1992). I have read this book and spoken with Alan and strongly suggest this book to all who are interested in patents and especially to those who are independently pursuing a patent separately from their primary occupation.

INNOVATION

An innovation is really the application of an invention or an idea. It can be small or large depending on whether it is an improvement to a particular product, process or a major breakthrough.

Actually, what seem to be major innovations are sometimes the result of a series of small innovations. Well, not really small innovations but small*er* innovations. For example, we had the telephone invented and then along came digital transformation and transportation of information. These, and a series of relatively minor innovations brought the fax machine of today. No one sat back 70 or 80 years ago and said "I think I will invent a fax machine." The inventions and innovations just described led to the fax not as an innovation, but as a result of previous innovations.

TECHNOLOGY

Today, we link science and technology because of the many science based technological developments. However, technology does not, or at least did not, always refer to any connection with science. 100, 200 and 300 years ago in agricultural societies, the change in shape of a particular earth moving tool—an innovation so to speak—could result in what could be called a new technology. Certainly, the modifications of certain farming tools to be pulled by animals resulted in a new technology, and, in more recent times, the mechanization of these tools into earth movers and tractors and so on resulted in different technologies.

Now, linking technologies with science, digital electronics, as mentioned above, is something to be considered as a new technology. At this time, we have science based industries which are based on chemistry, physics, molecular biology, and mathematics. The computer is probably the most prominent technological development of our time.

The basketball used by the National Basketball Association (NBA) used to be made out of leather. Now, it is actually a composite of various materials specifically designed to give the same "bounce" but to have much more durability and to last much longer. This applies to the basketballs sold in sporting goods stores for general sports, in addition to the NBA. So you see, modern technology by virtue of computers, new composite materials, electronics, chemistry, physics, and more is all around us and is part of our society today. Here, rather than to lock ourselves into a particular definition of technology, we have explored what it is and what it encompasses. If you "feel" you know what it is—you can help advance it.

CHAPTER 11

Quality Control

One of the first things that a person should realize about quality control is the difference between Quality Control and Quality Assurance. Sometimes the difference is only slight and sometimes the difference is very great. It depends on the company, the company's products, the company's philosophies, and the company's size.

Generally speaking, Quality Assurance is the overall quality function which includes Quality Control. The quality assurance department determines what is necessary to satisfy the customer with regard to all the attributes associated with the products, and sets up specifications or requirements that must be met by the product in order to *assure the quality*.

Quality Control, on the other hand, has the responsibility of sampling the product and conducting tests, the results of which will indicate whether or not the product is going to assure the customer of the quality that the customer expects.

In a very small company, say only a few persons, maybe 10 or 20, a particular individual can have a primary assignment involving production, and can also be the quality assurance person and the quality control person. Frequently, this is the staff engineer.

In a company that may have up to 100 or 200 employees, there may be a separate quality assurance department which will include the quality control function, which may consist of one or possibly a few persons. Here again, a staff engineer or chemist or physicist may be directly involved in this.

In very large companies, there are separate quality assurance departments or divisions which may include, or may be separated from, somewhat huge quality control departments or divisions.

In this chapter, we will assume that the quality assurance function has already determined what attributes are necessary to give satisfaction to the customer and we will speak primarily of the quality control function as it measures and/or controls the quality associated with the product.

WHAT IS THE VALUE OF QUALITY
TO THE CONSUMER?

In today's society, the consumer determines the quality level that is most satisfactory, and there are lot of these levels. For instance, what determines the quality of a suit? It is a combination of the fabric itself, the quality of the sewing, the fit, the appearance when the person is wearing the suit, and possibly some other factors that you may think of about your suits that you are concerned with when you purchase a suit. In a more general form, the materials, the workmanship, and the combination of these as exhibited in the finished product seem to determine the quality to the consumer. However, one person may be content with a $200 suit while another purchases a $400 suit and still another desires a $1,000 suit. Is the $1,000 suit 5 times as good as the $200 suit? Maybe on an individual materials plus workmanship basis that 5 times factor does not directly come into play, but, to the person who has the money to spend on a $1,000 suit, it is worth 5 times as much as the $200 suit.

Let's look at cars for a moment. Is a $200,000 Rolls Royce 20 times as valuable as a $10,000 Toyota Tercel? To the Rolls Royce owner it is, otherwise he would not have purchased it. To the Toyota Tercel owner, it isn't (or maybe it is and this person just hasn't achieved that level of income yet).

How about a Rolex watch? You can buy a watch that is accurate to plus or minus 5 minutes a day for $20. You can buy a watch that is within a few seconds/day for $100 or $200. Why would you spend $5000 on a Rolex? Well, some people feel that it is worth the price. If your income is in the range of the typical Rolex buyer's income, you may very well feel it is worth $5,000 also. Certainly, there are many people that do because the company is selling enough watches to make a good profit.

So you see, quality is in a large part dependent on your customer, what the customer expects of the product, and more specifically, what the customer expects of the various attributes of the product that comprise the overall product performance.

PRODUCE THE BEST YOU CAN
POSSIBLY PRODUCE!

Often, you will hear people say "Make the best product you possibly can." That is a very good statement to make and it ranks up there with the

American flag, motherhood, and apple pie. However, it is not always practical to produce the best you possibly can produce. While this is the technical part of this book, we begin to realize that we are intimately connected with many parts of the business function, and at this particular point, we begin to realize that the marketing function plays a part here. The part is that of satisfying the customers after having determined the customers needs. If your company has determined that *your customer* in the demographic profile toward which your company is selling has a particular quality level in mind, then *your product* should be directed toward that quality level. It may be possible for you to produce a higher quality level. This however, will cost you a lot more money to produce and you may end up pricing yourselves out of the market in the segment to which your market is directed. For example, if you are marketing cars in the under $10,000 price range, i.e., you have determined that that is the segment of the market that you want to sell to, you are not going to run tests to ensure that every engine produced will be good for 300,000 miles. Most people purchasing a car that costs under $10,000 understand that they may not get 300,000 miles from that car. On the other hand, Mercedes owners can expect mileage greater than 300,000 from their car, and Mercedes Benz designs the product and tests accordingly to ensure that this is the type of product that people in their market segment believe they are purchasing and in fact will receive.

When you design your quality control tests they should be designed to test for the quality level that is associated with your product and that quality level should be known before the product is ever manufactured. This is to say that the quality level should be known or desired before actual mass production. Sometimes after the product comes on the mass production line, quality levels may have to be adjusted somewhat when they are found that they either cannot be met in the current production line or that they are very easily met.

WHAT CHARACTERISTICS WILL YOU TEST FOR?

You design your tests to find the quality level as reflected in certain characteristics. Those characteristics are:

- Level of quality
- Consistency in meeting that level

Let's give an example here. In Chapter 6 on statistics, we discussed the normal distribution. It is also called a gaussian, or a bell shaped distribution. Let's look now as though you are a manufacturer selling bottles of juice. You are filling the bottles up to 28 ounces with juice. There is a "head space" available for air space and, it will actually permit a little bit of overfill. You desire however, to fill exactly 28 ounces in the bottle. Figure 11-1 illustrates that you are averaging 28 ounces and that you have a rather narrow distribution about that average 28 ounces. That is, you are filling a few with a little more and an equal number with a little less. This is a pretty good distribution, so you are achieving your quality (as reflected here and defined as being the quality for your production system in filling the desired 28 ounces). You are filling exactly what you want to fill and you have a narrow, that is good, distribution about that average.

Look now at Figure 11-2. This shows that you are right on the average of 28 ounces and you are filling an equal number low as are high, however, your range is much wider. Then you are filling some way over the desired 28 ounces and some way under the desired 28 ounces. You are filling an equal number either way but your system should be "tightened up a bit."

Figure 11-3 shows that your system is skewed to the left. This is to say that you have a rather narrow distribution indicating your system is running well in that regard, but, almost everything is being filled on the low side and therefore, in reality, is not being filled. You have a narrow distribution about a low value. This is not desirable.

Another way of presenting your data is to present it on a chart as illustrated in Figure 11-4. Here, the horizontal axis would reflect the number of samples or production items and the vertical axis would have placed on it the desired number and would have above it a line drawn as an UPPER CONTROL LIMIT (UCL), and would have a line drawn below the desired value listed as LOWER CONTROL LIMIT (LCL). You would plot your sample values on this chart and get a scatter diagram showing how well your system is running. This is a different way of presenting your data instead of as is shown in Figures 11-1, 11-2, and 11-3.

We have just looked at accuracy and consistency of that accuracy with regard to numerical values as obtained within a manufacturing system. We also did something like that in Chapter 6 on Statistics.

Keep in mind however that with any system you must still consider accuracy and consistency of that degree of accuracy, whether it is defined by numbers as we have shown here or whichever way you define it.

Remember also, that you want to keep track of the accuracy and the consistency of that accuracy with regard to various attributes about your product, not just one single attribute.

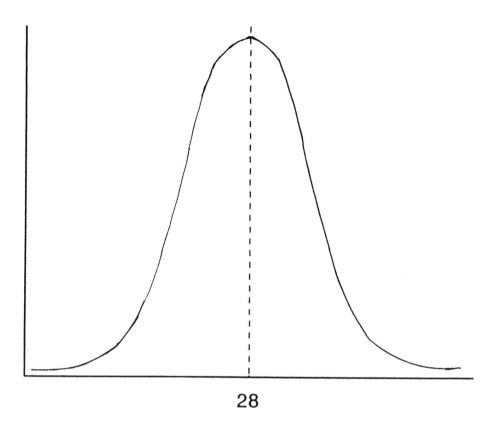

28

Figure 11-1.

TOTAL QUALITY MANAGEMENT (TQM)

This has been mentioned in Chapter 6. Essentially, TQM refers to everyone in the organization having a dedication toward quality, both to the final purchaser and consumer, and to the next person in the "production line" of the company. Production line is referred to here as every person in the company from the CEO, through the research and development persons, through the sales and marketing persons, up to and including the shipper at the shipping dock, instead of simply "sorting out the bad ones" at the regular production line. TQM involves minimizing the inferior products that are produced. Actually, the goal is to have no inferior products produced.

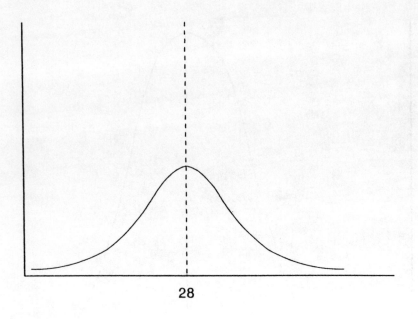

28

Figure 11-2.

We mentioned in Chapter 6 that there are several consultants getting a lot of money to put this principal into place. Actually, if you practice that in everything you do, in your job and in all phases of your life, you can have a very rewarding life.

MALCOLM BALDRIGE

The Malcolm Baldrige Award is given by the Federal Government to various companies each year to honor their excellence in Quality Assurance and Quality Control. Malcolm Baldrige was our 26th Secretary of Commerce, having been nominated by President Ronald Reagan in 1980 and confirmed by the United States Senate in 1981. During his time as Secretary of Commerce, he was considered to have accomplished much. He is considered to have been a very good manager and a colorful personality. He was an avid horseman and earned several awards on the rodeo circuit. Malcolm Baldrige died in July, 1987 in a rodeo accident. Soon after, the Reagan administration initiated the Malcolm Baldrige Award

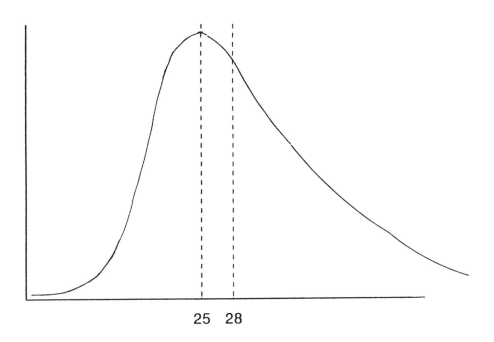

25   28

Figure 11-3.

to be given annually to various companies who have shown dedication to quality for the customer.

DIFFERENT VIEWS ON QUALITY COSTS

There are some companies who believe that not only can extremely high quality levels be reached, but that in reaching these levels, costs can be reduced. This is to say that the highest quality actually costs less for the manufacturer rather than more, as is commonly believed.

Motorola, a winner of the Malcolm Baldrige Award for quality, has very high goals and believes that attainment of their goal will actually reduce

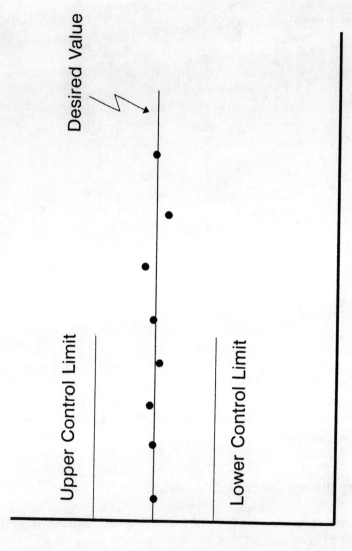

Figure 11-4.

costs. Paul Noakes, Vice President and Director of Quality Programs at Motorola is very convincing in conversations on the subject and was kind enough to forward much literature to me on their goal and their plans to achieve it.

What is Motorola's goal? It is formidable! They are at, or approaching, the end of a 5 year project to have 6 sigma (6 σ) quality. In Chapter 6, we showed that a 3 σ quality level indicated that 99.7% of all the parts that we wanted to make correctly were in fact made correctly. That 99.7% really is 99.73%. That means that out of every 1,000,000 parts produced 997,300 will be good. That also implies that 2,700 will be defective. The 99.7% does not sound so good when you view it this way. Motorola views it this way. 6 σ quality means that there are less than 4 parts per million defective when that level (6 σ) is achieved. The actual number is 3.4. Arithmetically, 3.4 defects may occur out of every 1,000,000 parts produced. Saying this again, when the 6 σ level is achieved 999,996 parts out of every 1,000,000 have been produced at the desired quality level. 4 or less have been unsatisfactory.

The other side of the coin was presented in a September 7, 1992 Newsweek article titled "The Cost of Quality," by Jay Mathews and Peter Ketel (pp 48-49). This interesting article mentions that "faced with hard times, business sours on 'total quality management'." In the article, they give an example where a company was so obsessed with improving its inventory process that it spent a fortune on a state-of-the-art computer system with the result that the wholesale cost of producing a 25 cent item "soared to a ridiculous $2.89." They mentioned that in current times the cost of quality is being questioned.

The two different and opposing points of view presented above represent an interesting polarity. What do you do? Well, you have to look at your product, your company, your philosophy, your customers, and the costs of your quality level that you decide to achieve. This book can not tell you what level you should achieve. Only you can determine what level you want to seek. Certainly, Motorola is the creme de la creme and I emphasize the courtesy and the sincerity that came across in my discussions with Paul Noakes. Ultimately, you must take the points of view that are presented here and determine what is most appropriate for your product.

CHAPTER 12

Technical Service

Technical Service means different things to different companies. We will try here to determine, in a sense, what it sounds like it should be. Actually, for some companies, Technical Service is whatever they want it to be. Sometimes, it's a catchall for activities that don't fit into other categories. So, what is Technical Service in your company? What do you want it to be in your company? What is the difference between your Customer Service and your Technical Service?

DEFINING TECHNICAL SERVICE

You may want to answer the above questions for yourself and your company. Let's say here that the technical service function (person, department, division, etc.) is that function which serves others within, and possibly outside of the organization with regard to the technical aspects of the product or the process by which the product is made. This would differentiate it from Customer Service per se in the sense that Customer Service normally applies to nontechnical or very slightly technical aspects of a product for the general consumer. Technical Service, as we have defined here, emphasizes in its activity, both words of the department name, Technical and Service. Let's look for a minute at to whom the technical service function responds. An examination of Figure 12-1 shows that your technical service can be external or internal. If external, it is usually performed for your customers. Some activities can be performed by governmental agencies, and these can be considered part of Technical

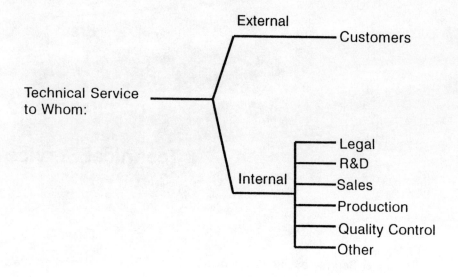

Figure 12-1.

Service, but these are usually set up as different entities such as Regulatory Affairs, and are coordinated through the legal department of your company. So if they are coordinated through the legal department of your company, you can consider that legal department your internal customer. As you see upon reviewing the internal customers that may use the services of the technical service department, you have your own company's legal department, research and development section, sales department and others as illustrated.

Why is this important to define? Because, if you have a technical service department and you don't define what it does, you will find that everyone is calling upon the technical service function to help them and you may be overwhelming that department by permitting them to be overloaded with work, very little of which contributes to making a better product or generating sales. Therefore, it is fitting that you determine what your technical service function is going to do and for whom it is going to do it. In Figure 12-1, we can define the various departments for whom technical service will exist. What is it going to do is another question. With regard to what is it going to do, it can perform preventive functions.

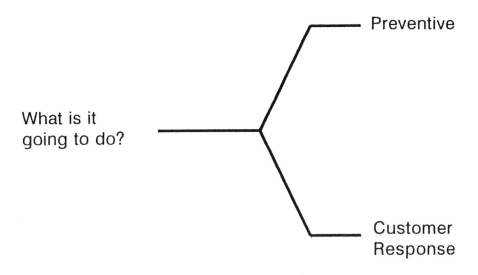

Figure 12-2.

It can investigate the potential problems with a product or process and make corrections before they become real problems. Here now, there is a very narrow line—depending on your company and your product—between the technical service activity and your research and development activity.

If you are going to respond to customers, and we are referring to any of the several customers listed in Figure 12-1, you must be ready to respond to those needs—usually rather rapidly.

What does it matter if you define whether the work will be preventive in nature or in response to a customer problem? Well, when you are in response to a customer problem, speed is of the essence. When the work is preventive in nature, there is usually a little more time available. This makes a big difference in how you set up your department with regard to work schedules. (See Figure 12-2.)

Think also about the customer contact. We are speaking here of any of the customers, both internal and external, that have been listed in Figure 12-1. Will a technical service person be permitted to speak with and correspond with an external person without having a salesperson present? This is done occasionally, but most of the time this is not done. The sales people want to be involved if you are dealing with their customers. Regarding external customer contact, will a technical service person travel to customers with a salesperson so that the problem can be identified firsthand? Some policy should be established that is a company wide policy or is each individual sales person's policy. It seems that the best relationship would always be for the sales person and the technical service person to function as a team. That way, the sales person won't say the wrong thing about the technical aspects of the product nor will the technical service person say anything to the customer that the salesperson doesn't want said.

What relationship is the best? This book can't tell you that. You must determine which is best for your company based on your product and your customer.

There is another question to be answered. To whom should the head of Technical Service report? Should that person report to, say, the Vice President of Operations or the Vice President of Technology? Before we answer that question, let's look at another aspect of the situation. You have to first figure out if your Technical Service function is using expensive equipment, like mass spectrometers and things of that nature. If this is the case, then you must determine if your Research and Development department has that equipment and if your Technical Service function is going to use the same equipment. The reason for this is that if your Research and Development department has purchased this equipment out of its budget and the Technical Service department uses that equipment, and the Technical Service department reports to the Vice President of Operations, then the Vice President of Technology to whom the Research and Development department reports may not care too much for that situation. They may feel that their equipment is being used by the Technical Service function on some unnecessary projects.

On the other hand, if such equipment is used by both Technical Service and Research and Development, it must be determined whether it is reasonable to buy the same equipment for each. In most cases, it is usually not feasible to have duplication of equipment. Please note that in some cases it is feasible to have duplication of equipment. We are saying here that in most cases it is not. So you see, you have to determine first who is going to use whose equipment and who is paying for the equipment and the types of projects that will be handled by the department (actually the types of projects that will be handled determine the equipment that will be needed) before determining to whom the department should report.

SUMMARY

In summarizing this relatively short chapter, no attempt has been made to present the ideal solution for your company. You can determine that after you consider the following items:

- The nature of the product
- The nature of the problems to which the Technical Service department will respond
- To whom (internal or external customers) the Technical Service department will respond
- How much time to respond will be available, which in turn will depend on whether the function is preventive or direct response to an internal or external customer...and these are not mutually exclusive, it can be both.
- What equipment will be used
- Will this equipment be shared by or owned by another department
- To whom should the technical service department report

Consideration of the above factors will assist you immensely in determining the size, the assignments, and the actual set up of your Technical Service department. Consider these factors and you will set up your Technical Service department or modify the one you already have to make it more satisfactory to your customers and to you.

CHAPTER 13

Research and Development

In this chapter on research and development, we will address such issues as:

- What is research and development?
- Why is it needed? (If in fact you believe it is needed.)
- How does research and development relate to the rest of a company?
- Laboratory structures.
- Difference between research and development and technical services.
- How to direct research and development.
- Chain of command for research and development in a company.

To answer the question of "what is research," we would first say that it is exploring new things.   Certainly, in Star Trek, the Enterprise is on a research function going "... where no man has ever gone before." This is research, indeed.   However, many of us are involved in research about more worldly pursuits.

In a sense, development is a stage of research. You could, if you wish, break research down into basic research and applied research and then into development and so on. This is done for you in Table 13-1.

A review of Table 13-1 will show that as we increase from basic research up to production, the probabilities associated with what we are going to learn increase significantly. We are not sure what we are going to get out of basic research, and then we have more predictability associated with applied research, and then more as we go down the chart.

Table 13-1 shows the various classifications of research and even includes production under the heading of research. As you review this table, you may choose other words to describe what occurs within your

Table 13-1.

Type of Classification	What it is	Output
Basic research	A scientific investigation of some phenomenon without a definite realization of what practical application will come from it.	Knowledge
Applied research	An investigation into knowledge, new or old, that already exists, in an effort to find particular applications of that knowledge.	Knowledge directly related to specific applications.
Development	Further exploration and testing of a potential application to determine the feasibility of a new product or process.	A product model or process system model and the feasibility and/or probability associated with it.
Pilot Plant	The testing of a product or process using the specifications that emerged from the development stage.	Economic feasibility , i.e., the costs likely to be associated with this product or process when in production.
Production, initial	The designing and implementation of production equipment for this new process or product with the testing and adaptation until satisfactory running of the system is attained...or the decision is made to cease the system.	The complete operational system.

company, but this chart should give you a good overview of the types of research and why, here, development is considered a stage of research.

Certainly, all companies don't engage in all aspects of research and development. There are not too many companies that engage in Basic Research. There are some, however, but not too many.

Another thing to consider is the source of research. It does not have to come from your own company. In Figure 13-1, we see that industry conducts research, the federal government conducts research, and academia conducts research. With each of these sources, there is a variety of research that is done. Industries conduct research on various products and processes characteristic of the individual company. Of course, as a company, you probably don't want to ask a competitor to do research for you. Once you tell your competitor your ideas, there would be a short time interval between the time of the telling of your goals and the day that your competitor becomes very large and your company goes out of existence. However, smaller companies with strong research aspects have been purchased by larger companies to become divisions of larger companies. Do not rule this out.

The federal government has various agencies associated with it and many of them conduct research into areas directly related to that agency. In most cases, the information obtained is readily available to the general public.

Academia conducts much research. Think of what area you want research performed in and then go to some university that is associated with that (for example, an agricultural college if your company is in that line of business, etc.) and get to know the professors who have graduate students working for them doing research. In many cases, sometimes associated with a grant from your company, the research projects assigned to the graduate students can be directly associated with knowledge you are seeking, and the knowledge will be made available to your company before the general publication. I am not saying here that private industry should control the research associated with projects for graduate students, but I am saying that in many cases there is no conflict whatsoever, and it is an intelligent way of getting the information you need. Your company wins, the college wins, and the graduate student wins.

As you observe Figure 13-1, you see the arrows point in different directions. When you view it in this manner, you can see the many options available to you for obtaining research information. An aspect to consider however, is that when you contract out for research, as you give the research agency with whom you are contracting the freedom to do the

RESEARCH

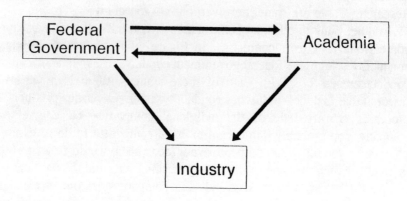

Figure 13-1.

research, you are giving up some of the control you would have within your own organization.

WHY IS RESEARCH AND DEVELOPMENT NEEDED?

Research and development is needed in order to keep up with the times, or in fact, to keep ahead of the times. Now, if your company manufactures golf tees or clothes pins you may question the need for extensive research, and justifiably so. On the other hand, if you can improve on these traditions you can probably make a lot of money.

Let's look at some other industries. Suppose you manufacture manual typewriters and chose not to keep up with the change to electric and then to electronic and then to word processors. At this time, there are no manual typewriters being manufactured, at least not in the United States and probably not anywhere in the world. Let's look at another example, digital watches. Around 1967 and 1968, 90% of all watches were manufactured in Switzerland, and then in 1968, the digital watch was invented. People now could see the actual digits that would indicate the time of day. Initially, you had to push the little button in order to get the watch to light up. Subsequently, the watches have improved over the last

25 years and now you just look at them and time is displayed along with various other information, and, much more information can be presented at the touch of a button. The Swiss watch makers believed that people would not want to change and would prefer the former style—the way watches have always shown the time—and hence, did not immediately go into the digital watch. On the other hand, various companies in the United States started manufacturing digital watches. Today, just look around you and you will see how popular, and in fact commonplace the digital watch is. Some of the other styles are still being manufactured, but by far, a large portion of that market is the digital watch. Currently, about 20% of all the watches sold are manufactured in Switzerland. By the way, where do you think the digital watch was invented? If you haven't guessed, it was invented in Switzerland.

Here is another case. This is a situation where the company had the "research and development outlook" to find a new use for a previously rejected product. In the early 1970s, Upjohn discovered that its Minoxidil prescription drug which was taken by consumers to reduce hypertension caused a particular side effect. This side effect was excessive growth of hair. Looking at this side effect from a positive point of view, the scientists at Upjohn investigated various forms of the product while considering it primarily for the purpose of hair growth. In 1988, the product was put on the market as a pharmaceutical formulation that would aid hair growth. It was released under the trade name Rogaine. The sales of this product are in the vicinity of a quarter of a billion dollars.

So you see, whether you need research and development, or what degree you are going to engage in research and development, is up to you, your company, and the company's philosophies. Remember the board of directors, the CEO, and the president have the philosophies. They are expressed as the viewpoint and outlook of the company.

RESEARCH AND DEVELOPMENT AND THE REST OF THE COMPANY

Just where does research and development fit in with the rest of the company? Well, think back to Chapter 1 where we discussed business as a mobile. We said that each area of the business was connected to the other areas such as the individual items on a mobile. If the mobile is say, ships, and it is suspended from the ceiling at a central point and each of these ships that is subsequently suspended, however indirectly, from this central point is represented by research and development, manufacturing, sales, marketing, etc., we saw that any major change in one would bring or necessitate a shift from the others in order to maintain the equilibrium. In a business, you are continually trying to displace this equilibrium forward and then as one area changes, the other must change to accommodate it.

So where does research and development fit into the overall scheme? When research and development designs a new product or process, or improves an existing product or process, the areas of sales, marketing, manufacturing, and others, must adapt in order to maintain this shifting equilibrium. Let's take a case where research and development improves an existing manufacturing process thereby saving time and money. In a case like this, the company may chose to sell more of a particular item since it can now produce more of that particular item without any major capital expenditure. (They made the expenditure in paying for the research and development.) As such, sales and marketing must fall in line with the manufacturing process improvement that was designed by the research and development department.

Actually, no division, department or area stands alone in its own right. If it did, it would then be its own company quite possibly in competition with the company of which it is suppose to be a part. The essence of a business is for all of the parts to work in conjunction with each other.

LABORATORY STRUCTURE

In a small company, there may be no direct laboratory as such. In a small to medium size company, there may be a laboratory that performs research and development functions, technical service functions, and quality control functions all within the same laboratory space. Then, as companies get larger, the separation of quality control, technical service, and research and development becomes more distinct. We have chosen in this book to treat them as separate subjects. This is done in the larger companies.

The following refers to the big companies. Here again, we are not speaking of medium and large companies as defined by sales volume, because while that is good for stock exchange purposes for Wall Street, here we also have to couple the size of the company with the philosophies of the top management. As we have already mentioned throughout this book, you may have a company of a particular size that has a research and development oriented management and another company of the same size that is not research and development oriented. Therefore, you have the size of the company, the philosophies of the top management, and the nature of

ORGANIZATIONAL OPTIONS

LINE MANAGEMENT

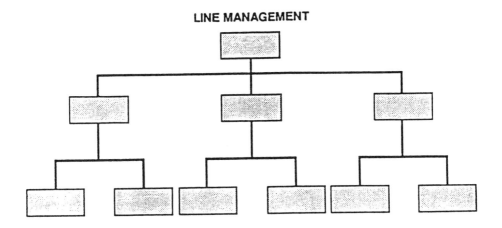

MATRIX/PROJECT MANAGEMENT

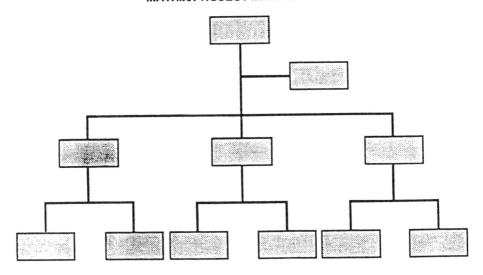

Figure 13-2.

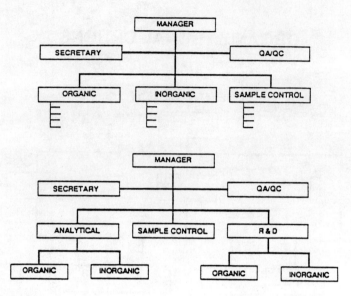

CHARACTERISTICS:

- CLEAR LINE OF COMMAND
- RESPONSIBILITY FOR PRODUCTION WELL DEFINED
- WORKS WELL FOR PRODUCTION TYPE WORK
- PROVIDES CLOSE SUPERVISION
- WORKING DIRECTLY FOR PERSON MOST INFLUENTIAL

Figure 13-3. Line Management

the products all determining whether research and development will or will not be a separate function. As a separate function, we mean here separate persons engaged in research and development as their primary job responsibility.

The two primary organizational operations utilized in a laboratory are line management, and matrix/project management, both of which are shown in Figure 13-2. The line management option is shown in more detail in Figure 13-3 and the characteristics of that option are shown immediately below the illustration. The matrix or project management option is depicted in Figure 13-4 with its characteristics shown below the illustration.

Observations of the figures show that for line management there is a clear line of command, however, this is best for a production type situation. Looking at the project management outline, we see that it is the best for research type activity. It also has the least direct supervision, a characteristic which is good for a research function. Research people do not like to be supervised too directly. However, we see that the project members have two bosses: the laboratory manager and the project manager. Another way

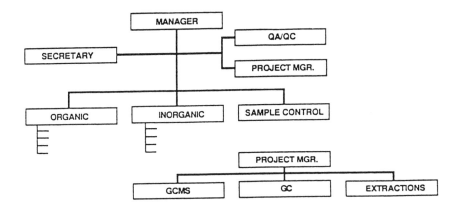

CHARACTERISTICS:
- MOST SENSITIVE TO CUSTOMER'S NEEDS
- SELECT INDIVIDUALS USED
- CLEAR RESPONSIBILITY FOR THE JOB
- BEST FOR RESEARCH TYPE ACTIVITY
- LESS DIRECT SUPERVISION
- PROJECT MEMBERS HAVE TWO BOSSES

Figure 13-4. Matrix/Project Management

of looking at this, and it is a way that exists in many places, is that the project manager may be a highly skilled research person that is directing the various laboratory people that are involved in a particular project, but, the laboratory people really directly report to the laboratory manager, who is the person who is responsible for their evaluations and their raises and all those good things. Where do you think their dedication is going to be? This is to say that the project management option looks like it works very well, and it can work very well, provided the sensitivities are taken into account first hand.

Your best system from an efficiency point of view is to have every single person in the laboratory have an entire range of their own equipment. That is idealistic. It usually cannot be afforded economically. Therefore, you will probably end up with some system like one or the other shown here.

Which system is best for you? Is it line, matrix, or some combination of the two? Only you can decide that, but now you know what types are available or are commonly used, and the characteristics or advantages and disadvantages of each.

DIFFERENCE BETWEEN RESEARCH AND DEVELOPMENT AND TECHNICAL SERVICES

Sometimes people wonder if there is in fact a difference between research and development and technical service. Well, there is. In small firms, as has already been mentioned, the two functions may be handled by the same individual or the same small group of individuals. In these firms, however, management may want to keep track of the research and development projects as distinct from the technical service projects for financial purposes, so that they can calculate their return on investment from each. This is especially true in a small growing company where management may want to expand one function but not necessarily the other. If the research and development projects have returned more in the line of new products and new process, or improved product and improved processes than did the technical service function return on the investment, then, the management of the company may wish to put more money into the research and development in order to make more money in the long run.

In a large company, the two functions are usually distinct with regard to personnel, that is, they usually consist of different persons or different groups of persons. Chapter 12 discussed the technical service function while this chapter is discussing the research and development function, and by now, it is hoped that the difference is clear. So generally, technical service applies to an existing product or process when there is some "troubleshooting" needed or when some "preventive" type attention is needed. The research and development function develops new products and processes or attempts to improve existing ones even when there is no apparent problem.

HOW TO DIRECT THE RESEARCH AND DEVELOPMENT FUNCTION

Directing the research and development function of a company is an exercise in people skills. Much more will be said about people skills in the last chapter of this book, however, some things should be said now especially on the subject of "research and development people." They are, in a way, a different breed.

There is a paradox here. A really good research and development person, or department, or division (let's for the sake of discussion here call it a department) can produce innovations that will result in huge income for the company. The paradox is that it is sometimes difficult to measure. Compare this to the sales function where a good sales department will go out and generate business. This business can be measured very readily by the actual amount of sales this year compared to the amount of sales last year.

Then you might say if the research and development department invents something new, the entire sales of that new thing were affected by the invention of that item by the research and development department. Research and development will agree with you, however, the sales department may not agree with you. So we get right down to the question of how do you measure the productivity of a research and development function. Here, we will say a little bit about how you measure productivity before actually going into how to direct the persons in research and development. It's always good to know what your product is and how you are going to measure the attainment of your goals, and then you can figure out how to direct the department toward those goals.

Really, how do you measure the productivity of your research and development department?

- The number of projects completed in a given time period:

  That does not really measure productivity; that simply measures the number of projects completed in a given time period.   The times measured in person/days required on a project can be very small. This is to say that a company can, in plain words, have a lot of little projects going at one time. This in turn does not mean that these projects are not productive. It depends on the nature of the business.

- The number of projects carried at a particular point in time:

  The answer to this is very similar to the above answer. Much of this depends on the nature of the business and the products or processes involved.

- The sales generated by the "inventions":

If you did not count any other department's contribution such as those of sales, marketing, manufacturing, etc., you could attribute the income as a measure of the success or productivity of the research and development department. It would not be a dollar for dollar comparison, but a good relative comparison of project to project could be made. This would be for the research and development that produced new products. It does not quite answer the question of how you measure the productivity of a project that was directed toward improving a process.

• The research and development Director's monthly report:

This is a small version of the President's annual report. The President never says "I fouled up a bit this year, but I'll try to do better next year." The President usually says something like "...due to fluctuations in the international monetary exchange and other global factors..." and then pads the rest of the text. You can not expect a research and development director to say much different in the report. A monthly report is expected to provide others with information regarding the progress and status of various projects. It should not be expected to be a primary factor contributing to the career demise of the director who wrote it.

The point here is that you can not measure the productivity of the research and development department as precisely as you can that of the sales department. Sales can be measured rather precisely—certainly as compared to measuring the productivity of a research and development department. Indeed, as precise as scientists like to be, in a research function the results can be measured in semi-quantitative terms like mediocre, good, very good, and excellent. When you're a research and development person, you are relying on faith and your track record.

Now, getting on to how to direct a research and development function. Realizing what we just stated above about measuring productivity, one obvious goal is to have so much productivity and so many great inventions that people will not have to talk in terms of dollars and cents—they will just know how good you are.

When managing or directing a research and development function, it is imperative to give the research and development people a high degree of freedom. Let's look at the characteristics of a research person. That person is:

• A positive thinker
• A daydreamer
• An explorer
• A person who requires much freedom

How do you manage this type of person? You give them an atmosphere that is conducive to positive thinking, daydreaming, exploring, and freedom. All this is, of course, within certain limits. The main point here is to realize that the research and development person must have more freedom and less direction than your production line person. This should seem obvious and this extreme comparison was presented just to illustrate the point. Even with scientists however, the research and development person should be given more freedom than the quality control person. The quality control person normally is expected to follow certain procedures, with the ability to modify those procedures at certain times in order to improve them. This occasional freedom that the QC person has is the type of freedom that the research and development person requires all the time.

Does this mean that you give a person an entire laboratory with an unlimited budget, deposit the paychecks in the bank for that person, and talk to them annually? No, it means that you listen to what they have to say and that you direct them at times a little more subtly and sometimes a little more firmly if they start to go a little more tangential to the goals of the company.

Directing a research and development function is in a large part a guiding and coaching type of managing.

You might wonder if you give freedom to a research and development person, will your researcher go way out and will you be wondering what's going on. That is unlikely, because, as much as a research person likes to do research, he also likes to let you know what he discovered. We all want recognition and a researcher is no exception. At a point in time, he will come up to you and in effect say "Look what I have discovered." This does not imply that you should sit back and wait until the researcher comes to you with discoveries. It is simply said so that you will see that you have not given up total control.

Have your periodic meetings and disseminate the information relevant to priorities and get the information back from your research staff, but do not keep tight reins on your staff and you will find that if they are true research and development people, you will have a productive department.

PART 3

INTEGRATING THE BUSINESS AND TECHNICAL AREAS FOR PROFIT

CHAPTER 14

The Corporation as a Unit:
An Overview

In Chapter 1, we discussed business in general and talked about various forms of business: corporation, partnership, and single proprietorship. Here, we are discussing the corporation as the unit, but actually separate from the terms that are used relevant to the corporation structure. The principles that are presented here apply to partnerships and sole proprietorships as well. The subjects that will be covered here are:

- The structure of the corporation
- Defining your business
- Goal setting and strategic planning
- Management styles

THE STRUCTURE OF THE CORPORATION

Let's take an analogy and compare the company to yourself. The company consists of various departments and we have studied several of these departments on an individual basis in the preceding chapters. However, they all exist at the same time and have interplay with each other (as we shall see to a greater degree in Chapter 15). We, as individuals, have various aspects of ourselves and our lives. We have our mental aspect, the way we think, read, learn, educate ourselves, and teach others. We have our religious aspect where we worship according to our choice and pray in accordance with our beliefs. We have our physical aspect, that is, how we look to ourselves and to others. We sometimes even go to a spa to work out, to build up that physical aspect. Yet, even though these are different aspects, they are really alive at the same time, like the departments or divisions within a company.

Our behavior will be in accordance with how we regard others and is very similar to the company's behavior being in accordance with the product that it wants to sell to its customers.

Refer now to Figure 14-1. You see the figure in two dimensions and you see the concentric circles. However, you can look at it that way or you can picture it as a sphere. Whichever way is most convenient for you is suitable here.

We see at the center of the circle the board of directors, the chief executive officer (CEO), and the president, as the people who control the company. They define the direction the company is to travel with regard to products and to markets.

We see, as we widen our view and make our picture more complete, the pie wedges represent various areas or departments or divisions. (We note here that if you, the reader, view this figure and believe that your area got "short changed" by either not being shown as a big enough wedge of the pie or not being included in the pie, just contact us and we will adapt this figure in the next edition. For example, management information service (MIS) was not omitted because it was not felt important; there are simply only so many areas that we selected to put in this drawing.)

We see now surrounding everything we have defined is a layer called shareholders. These are the stockholders who are part owners of the company. You are reminded that there are various classes of stock and different issues and that the primary types of stock are common and preferred. Most reporting is done based on the common stock issues. In any case, the shareholders own the company. They ultimately select the board of directors, which hires the CEO, who in turn hires the president. Therefore, the shareholders are pictured as surrounding the whole thing.

Now we see that there is another covering to the sphere or layer to the circumference of the circle. This is called stakeholder. A stakeholder is not necessarily a person who owns shares of stock but is a person or group of persons or agency of some kind to which the company has some sort of responsibility or interfaces with in some way. We see here that the neighbors of the manufacturing plant are stakeholders in the sense that they do not want their air polluted or their water supply harmed, or anything like that. The bank that the company borrows from is a stakeholder in the sense that money is owed to this bank. It is not a shareholder in the sense that

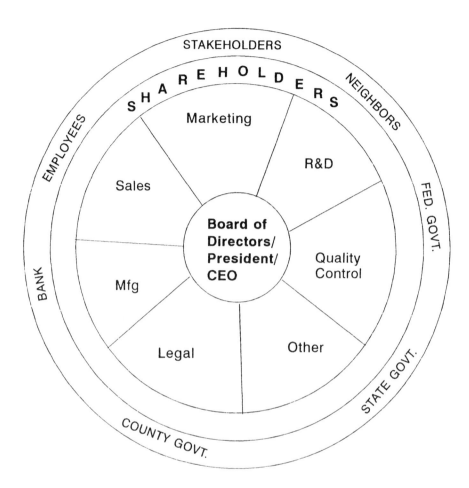

Figure 14-1.

it does not directly own the company or have any kind of ownership in the company. It is indeed a stakeholder in the sense that the company has to express concern about the bank with regard to paying its existing loans and keeping on good terms to get future loans. The other banks in the area who want to get business and beat out the bank that has the company's business are stakeholders in that respect. The various governments— county, state, and federal—are stakeholders in the sense that they have regulations with which the company must comply.

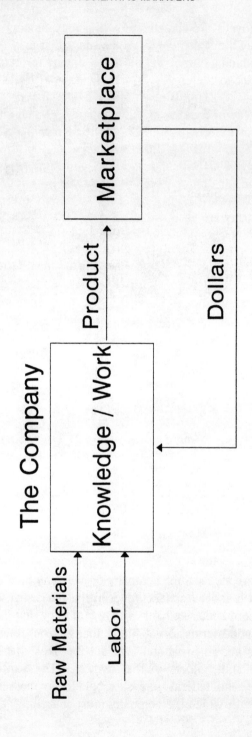

Figure 14-2.

The employees are stakeholders who may or may not also be share-holders. They are stakeholders in the sense that they are working for the company producing output and receiving money for it, and while they have a responsibility to the employer, the company also has a responsibility to them.

Another way of looking at the company is in Figure 14-2. We see in the figure that the company takes input of raw materials and labor and combines it with knowledge and work, and the outflow is represented by the word PRODUCTS. These products go to the marketplace where they are exchanged for dollars which are then fed back into the company. We know from Chapter 4, "Finance," that the dollars from sales that go back into the company are used initially to pay for the "cost of goods sold" and then to pay interest on bonds or loans and then to pay taxes, after which we have profit. This profit is going to either or both of two places: the shareholders, (owners in the form of dividends) and/or back into the company to buy new equipment or build new buildings, or things like that.

We have seen that the shareholders are the actual owners of the company and that the Board of Directors and the CEO and the President and in many cases the Chief Operating Officer (COO) actually run the company. What are the responsibilities of these persons—the CEO, the COO, and the President? Has anyone ever seen job descriptions for these persons? Well, let's look into what the respective responsibilities are for these executives.

A friend of mine, Jim Egan, who is a former corporate executive and now a corporate consultant, defined the duties of corporate executives as follows:

Chairman of the Board

The Chairman of the Board of Directors actually runs the show. Remember, the board of directors directs the activities of the company for, and in response to, the shareholders. The Chairman of the Board is, as the name of implies, the head of the Board of Directors. Traditionally, the Chairman of the Board was an employee of the company, in many cases a president of a company who moved up to become the Chairman of the Board. Nowadays, the Chairman of the Board of Directors is, like the other directors, a person who is not an employee of the company, but holds that position on the board of directors, specifically, Chairman. This accounts for the reasons why, in today's corporate structure, there are some "cleaning house" procedures when a new chairman takes over. The "good old buddy" situation that could develop between the chairman and the Chief Executive Officer and the President, when they all share the same country club membership does not hold true here. Of course, in many cases, the "good old buddy" system just evolved, and was not always meant to be that way. At a subconscious level, the executives would avoid confrontation with each other in the actual management of the company. Having the new Chairman of the Board as described above should preclude that.

Chief Executive Officer

The Chief Executive Officer (CEO) reports to the Chairman of the Board and has the President and the Chief Operating Officer (COO) reporting to him. The CEO, in effect, runs the company on a day-to-day basis. While the Chairman of the Board of Directors prescribes the directions of the company, the CEO executes the directions and actually manages the entire company.

Chief Operating Officer

The COO is in charge of the operating divisions of the company. These are the manufacturing divisions of the company. The COO would not have accounting, legal, and human resources divisions reporting to him. He is concerned with the actual production divisions.

President

The President has the legal, accounting, human resource, and other departments reporting to him.

The CEO, COO, and President, are not always three different persons. In some companies, they are. In this case, they have a peer type relationship but even with this, the CEO is the top gun. In other companies, the CEO and President are the same person. Still, in other companies the CEO, the COO, and the President are the same one single person. It depends a lot on the size of the company and whether the company is centralized or decentralized. In a decentralized company, there will be a trend to have the three distinctly different positions. In a centralized company, these can be combined much more readily. In yet another case, there may be a CEO and a President, and no COO—the President has that responsibility and may or may not have that title in addition to the title of President.

DEFINING THE BUSINESS

Periodically, the company must ask itself *What business are we in?* This may sound simple, but it is overlooked many times.   The classic answer of a person who wants to appear smart, but really is not too smart is "We are in business to make money." That is not really answering the question.

This is especially true in today's era of diversification. Some companies are diversifying and are being very successful at it. Take for example Phillip Morris, a cigarette manufacturer who acquired Miller Brewing Company, or R.J. Reynolds, another cigarette manufacturer who became RJR and acquired Nabisco and became RJR Nabisco. These companies saw that in today's health conscious society, less people would be smoking, and therefore less cigarettes would be sold. Had they continued along their current route, their sales would have diminished significantly. However, each of them chose to acquire other companies, believing their own management could help these companies they acquired and survival would be ensured. It worked out well for these companies. However, in another case, a large company became diversified and then began to narrow itself back down. A case in point is General Mills. General Mills had this organizational mission for a number of years:

General Mills markets consumer goods and services in five principal business areas—consumer foods, restaurants, toys, fashion, and specialty retailing. The company is committed to competitive excellence and to maintaining leadership among consumer goods companies through a strategy of balanced diversification, aggressive consumer marketing, and sound positioning within each industry group.

General Mills Annual Report 1984

However, due to poor results with toys and fashion retailing, the firm decided to narrow its focus:

General Mills is now a highly focused company with leadership positions in very profitable segments of the consumer foods and restaurant industries, plus a profitable and promising specialty retail business.

General Mills Annual Report 1985

So you see, you have to periodically ask yourself "What business are we in?"

Try, for an exercise, to pretend you are KODAK and ask yourself what business are you in.

- Film
- Videotape
- Image reproduction
- Image transmission
- Any other thoughts you may have to add to this list

The way you define your business is how your thinking will be directed. So you see, once you define your business, your thinking will be directed along the lines of your business as you have defined it. And while you may consider other aspects of your business in a diversification mode, you still will direct all your activities toward the prosperity of your business.

GOAL SETTING AND STRATEGIC PLANNING

In Chapter 1, we briefly mentioned the planning process and we said "If you do not know where you are going, how will you ever know when you get there?" Let's look first at the five fundamental steps in planning:

- Where do you want to go?
- What does it take to get there?
- Make the decision.
- Implement (do it).
- Monitor, feedback.

There are some who, when referring to strategic planning, call the assessment of an enterprise's capabilities and limitations a WOTS UP analysis. This is an acronym for **W**eaknesses, **O**pportunities, **T**hreats, and **S**trengths **U**nderlying **P**lanning. It is a nice acronym as far as acronyms go, but it really leaves a bit to be desired. What it leaves to be desired is the nature of the strategic planning process.   What we are saying here is that it's correct but incomplete.

We are going to go into an outline that contains several categories. Before presenting it, some things should be mentioned:

A strategic plan is normally prepared covering a period of approximately five years.   This does not mean that it is prepared and not looked at again for five years!   If it is not looked at for a period of five years, there may not be a company to look at—the company may have gone out of existence during that time.   Actually, it is good to review the strategic plan quarterly, monitor the progress, and update it as necessary.   The fact that it covers five years does not mean that it will be five years before the next strategic plan is drawn up.   While reviewed quarterly or semiannually or at whatever period of time you wish, you may very well draw up another strategic plan, one year after the first one.   This is because "things change."   You must accommodate accordingly.

There are several categories to be presented in the example given here. In the example, the research and development division is contained as an item in its own right.   You may choose to highlight another department, or more departments, or no particular department.   You may also choose not to have as many divisions as illustrated in our example.   That is okay.   You have to prepare it the way you feel is best for your company.   This is to be presented only as an example.

While we are referring here to the strategic plan for a company, you can also design a strategic plan for a division or a department.   For example, you can draw up a three year strategic plan for your sales department.   You do whatever suits your area of responsibility in the company.

Here is the outline:

Preface
Mission
Objectives
Threats and opportunities
Weaknesses and strengths
Growth
Buildings and equipment
Personnel
Research and development
Closing comments

Now that you have seen the outline, let's take the categories one by one.

Preface

This section should be relatively brief, only a paragraph or two. Say something to the effect of "This document contains the outline for ABC Company for the year (1993) through (1998).

"It is intended to be specific enough so that our lines of direction will be delineated: it will not be so specific that it takes away the freedom of some of the first levels of management.

"Additionally, it is realized that the internal and external environments are continually changing and with that in mind, this will not be regarded as an unchangeable document. It is intended to be officially reviewed on an annual basis, yet the changes could be made at any time depending upon what changes may occur in any of the factors discussed herein." You are just reminding the readers of the time period covered and that it can change as time goes on since everything in the world changes. Say it as informally as you wish.

Mission

Say here what your primary products are, and what rate of growth you desire, and how this will compare to previous times, i.e., will it be the same as or greater than in the past. Here again, a single paragraph tells the story.

Objectives

Your objectives will be something like:

A. Minimum 15% pre-tax profit
B. Minimum 15% return on average gross assets (ROAGA)
C. Maintain the high public image in the community
D. Maintain present market share of 25%

A-D, above can each contain one or two lines, which is about all that is necessary here.

Threats and Opportunities

Threats

Here, you could have such things as (depending on your product):

1. Product liability.
2. Governmental regulation.
3. Difficulty of continuing supply of certain raw materials.

You should say something about the expected effects of each.

Opportunities

In this section you can make statements that turn certain of the threats around. For example, you can state that product liability can be an asset to you if you believe you can have a safer product than your competitors are making. They will be more liable to lawsuits than you will be, and here you can list product liability as an opportunity. You can also include such things as customers relying on you for Technical Service, and this represents an opportunity to expand existing accounts.

Weaknesses and Strengths

Here are examples:

Weaknesses

1. No definitive measure of productivity.
2. Few or no patented products at a time when copying by competitors can be done with relative ease.
3. Little experience and expertise in a field which we want to enter.

Strengths

1. Considerable knowledge, experience, and technical expertise in our primary field of endeavor. Generally recognized as the leader.
2. Strong market knowledge.
3. Modern manufacturing equipment in a new plant.

Growth

Following is sample text.

1. Production—We will grow with plant #4 coming onstream next year. It is intended to maintain productivity from every square foot of manufac-

turing area, and in that regard, we are studying the repositioning of workflow in our plants.

2. Assets—Two new widget makers (large machines) each capable of producing 20 widgets/hour are scheduled for purchase next year.

3. Sales—We anticipate that this will grow at a rate of 15% per year based on the increase in our existing customers' needs and the expansion of their product lines. (Note to reader: This is of course relevant to you selling products for further manufacture by other companies. If you sell your widgets to the final consumer then this would be worded differently based on the consumer market itself.)

4. Profits—The increase in profits will be commensurate with the increase in sales and would grow at a rate of 15% pre-tax. With the consideration of an international market, there may be a potential for greater profit.

Buildings and Equipment (Optional Section)

This is an example you might use.

1. Buildings—Here you may care to list any buildings or sites that are used for research, manufacturing, conferences, or whatever by the company.

2. Equipment—Here you may care to itemize the equipment that is used in manufacturing, or in your research if you are a research oriented company, etc. This serves to give you a picture of where you are. Of course, this entire section is optional and many persons do not even consider such a section as this in their strategic plan.

Personnel

These are sample suggestions.

A. Existing personnel—At this time we believe we have highly qualified individuals in most sections of the administrative, technical, and manufacturing areas.

B. Training—We shall, through liaison with human resource development, continue to provide training to existing personnel. As individual assignments expand or as persons transfer from one assignment to another, if a need for training is determined to exist, it will be provided.

C. New personnel—We strive to attract above average people regardless of age, race, sex, color, creed, or national origin.

D. Intentions—We plan to keep our pay scales and fringe benefits above average in each area in which we operate.

We intend to provide clean, comfortable, and safe working conditions for factory and salaried employees. We will have employee-management meetings to discuss mutual problems, exchange ideas, and we will encourage participation in company sponsored affairs. We intend to provide an atmosphere where all employees will strive to use their talents and abilities to the fullest extent possible. We will do this by determining through our own observations, and through our human resources department, what is needed to satisfy the various needs of the employees. Satisfaction of these needs will encourage utilization of their talents and abilities to the fullest extent.

Research and Development

This is a sample statement.

We shall continue to maintain our emphasis on research and development efforts. This shall be done by carefully observing the market needs and by allotting funds and personnel to the research and development efforts. These efforts will be especially important as we pursue new areas for diversification, that is, into fields that are new to us.

Along with the emphasis on research and development, will be another aspect that is just as important—the conveyance of research findings to other personnel and the implementation of research findings to the production area and to the marketplace. This communication of the research findings is as important as the research findings themselves.

In addition, we shall, with the help of human resource department, instill a "research and development thinking" type attitude into those who are not considered research personnel, so that they will ask "How can we do it better?"—a question that should be present all of the time.

Closing Comments

This is an example summary.

It is believed that the contents of this document have served to tell not only what we anticipate doing the next five years but, as it should be in strategic planning, to tell how we are going to do this. As we plan for the next five years, there are two key factors. They are to set down the plan as best as it can be made at this time, and to monitor the progress and make changes whenever necessary. Such changes may be necessitated by changes in the internal or external environments. Surely, if anyone sets down a five year plan and does not monitor its progress or monitor the outside environment, the plan will become stale and useless. By monitoring the plan and making changes when necessary, the continual series of modified plans will help the division achieve its goals.

Efforts will be made to accurately measure what we call "productivity." This is the key word in most industries today. However, to say it is one thing and to measure it is another. We will think about measuring productivity as a ratio of sales to the number of employees. It can also be measured in dollars of profits divided by the number of employees. Maybe it should be measured in number of units shipped per square foot of production area. We will look into these various aspects to determine which of these or any others that we can think of will measure that which we continually seek to improve—productivity.

SUMMARIZING THE STRATEGIC PLAN

Surely, the strategic plan presented above contains a large number of categories. Certainly the last four sections of the plan are optional to many readers. The last three sections, personnel, research and development, and closing comments, in popularity and altruism, rank up there up with the big three: the American flag, motherhood, and apple pie.

You could say something like, "You put all great and wonderful things in that strategic plan but how in the real world are we going to carry out something like that?" Well, what goals do you want to set for yourself and your company? Admittedly, the wording in the last few sections of this strategic plan was very flowery. You may choose to have only the first few sections in your strategic plan and you may choose to be much more direct. Good for you! That is the way it should be!

The primary point here is to show what is included in a strategic plan and to show that the strategic plan does not have to be 100 pages long. The fundamental strategic plan as presented here could be only a few pages long, quite likely with the incorporation of graphical projections of anticipated sales, anticipated income and anticipated number of employees, but the fact remains that this does not have to be a voluminous document. The golden rule that says "do unto others as you would have them do unto you" is a rather brief statement but it is a good thing to plan your life around. The Ten Commandments are relatively short but get right to the point of how we are expected to live. Here in the United States, the

Constitution is not a very lengthy document but for over 200 years our country has thrived by adherence to this document. So you see, your Strategic Plan does not have to be hundreds of pages.

Keep in mind the difference between *strategy* and *tactics*. Strategy defines the overall philosophy while tactics explains the individual means of accomplishing the goals. As each division or department fashions its own strategic plan after the company's primary strategic plan, these individual plans will include more tactics that will define how the individual units of divisions or departments will accomplish their goals. Everything then blends upward to the overall company goal.

MANAGING

There are various management techniques, or ways of managing. Some of them are listed here:

- MBH. Management by Hiding. Here, the manager believes that if he cannot be found things will work themselves out. He will be around to take credit for things that his people do that help the company, but generally, this person lacks the nerve to face many of the problems that are associated with his department and can never be found. Needless to say, you do not want to be one of these and you do not want to work for one of these.
- Ostrich Management. This is very similar to MBH. However, just as the ostrich sticks his head in the sand and believes that he is hiding, this manager keeps on the move, and while he does not have a secret hiding place that no one knows about, he cannot be pinned down to answer questions or be faced with problems.
- Absentee Management. This is a technique used by managers that are never there. Many good managers travel a lot. The absentee manager is essentially traveling all of the time but no one knows where he is, how long he will be there, or when he will be back. This person is just "out."
- Mushroom Management. This is a technique used by some managers based on the principle used to raise mushrooms. This principal is keep the employees in the dark and throw manure on them.
- MBO. Management by Objectives. This is one of the more productive forms of management. Management by Objectives means the manager and an individual get together and list the objectives that the individual is to achieve in the next period of time, usually a year. The biggest problem experienced with this has been inflexibility. That is, the manager and the individual get together and set the objectives and then nobody

looks at them for a year, during which time business has changed, markets have changed, the world has changed, and the objectives have not changed. MBO works very well when flexibility is incorporated into the system: both in the initial setup of the objectives to be covered in the (usually) one-year time period and in the periodic (semi-annual or quarterly) review of these objectives to make them commensurate with the changing conditions within the company.

• MBCSN. This means managing by common sense and nerve. This principal coupled with getting out and seeing what is happening is the best form of management. Essentially, the manager does not sit at a desk behind a pile of computer printouts and get overwhelmed with statistics, but rather, gets out and sees what is going on in the company, talks to people in the company at all levels, discusses situations with other managers, uses common sense and has the nerve to make the proper decisions. This obviously is the type of manager you want to be and the type of manager you want to work for. It should be obvious that this last type of management presented is that type that will help the corporation forge ahead in achieving its goals.

CHAPTER 15

Business/Technical Relationships: The Symbiosis to Maximize Profits

There are times in some companies where the business functions and the technical functions seem to occupy two different worlds. Indeed, in some companies these worlds are constantly far apart. It is difficult to believe that a company is maximizing its profits when it has these two aspects of the corporation so widely apart.

This is not to say that they are feuding, but that they just don't seem to understand each other. How then do you get them to work better together? Well, you get them to try to understand each other. *That is a lot easier said than done!* However, just like with people that seem to be different than each other, trying to see things from another's point of view leads to an understanding of the other person even if not agreement with the other person's principles. So does an attempt at understanding another type of function in a company lead to an appreciation, if not an agreement with that other part of the company. This in turn should lead to some degree of symbiosis that will lead to maximizing the profits.

There are some companies where the technical and business functions "get along well." This happens often in small companies where the persons see each other on a daily basis. In larger companies that have maintained a relationship by education and by good, well planned, constructive meetings of the various disciplines this continues. Let's look at some typical topics or subjects and the comments that could possibly come from various departments or divisions. Let's look at a case in Table 15-1 where there is very little understanding among the various disciplines. Here, there are several blocks left empty. Rather than try to influence your opinion, you are invited to imagine what comments would fit in these blocks for

Table 15-1. Weak or Undesirable Relationship

Subject	R&D	Marketing	Legal	Sales	Manufacturing	Finance
New Product Design	This is a great new product. Let's hope that sales knows how to do a good job here so we can all get rich.	R&D did it again. They invented something no one will buy.	Wow! Those R&D people left this product open to liability suits. They never think of the legal end when they design something.		Oh Oh! They did it again! We have to retool the entire production line.	
Business Trips to Customers	We'd sell a lot more product if sales took us and our technical service people along on the business trips.		Don't let them talk to the customer. They'll promise them anything!	...now if those science people will just invent something else and do their own jobs we'll sell the products...		We're spending a lot of money sending unnecessary people on trips
New Production Equipment					At last.	Do they really need that?

Table 15-1. Continued

Subject	R&D	Marketing	Legal	Sales	Manufacturing	Finance
Advertising and Promotion	The company ought to spend a bundle on this—not that it needs it but because it's so good		We'd better be very careful what we say. We can be sued if we say the wrong thing.		Who cares!	Let's be careful what we spend.
New Product Testing		Let's get the data the minute it's available and run to the customer with it.		Let's get the data the minute it's available and run to the customer with it.		

your company (you can, if you wish, imagine a "worse case scenario," since you will be invited to do this again in Table 15-2 which will list some comments in a company with very good relationships).

You are encouraged to either draw up a chart similar to that in Table 15-1 and Table 15-2 with similar labels or make a copy of what's here and write in the empty blocks or overwrite the filled in blocks to see what fits for your company. If you do this and then take a close look at what you wrote, you will find the results to be very interesting regarding what the departments or divisions think of each other.

Let's go on to a company that enjoys very good relationships, perhaps exaggeratedly so for our example, but in any case, let's see what this would look like.

As we have seen, Table 15-1 depicts undesirable situations while Table 15-2 depicts a desirable, perhaps even a lofty, relationship. It would be great if your relationships were similar to that in Table 15-2 although, if they are somewhere in between 15-1 and 15-2 leaning toward the latter, then you're probably in pretty good shape. An example of some things that can happen when coordination between departments seems to be good but is not really understood well is as follows. In a case that I saw in industry, there was a manufacturer of rubber stoppers, the kind that go on medicine vials. These are very carefully designed so that little or none of the chemicals used in the manufacture of the rubber stopper extract into the prescription injectable solution and cause harm to the patient. A particular customer of the rubber stopper maker, a major pharmaceutical manufacturer, was very interested in a new formula stopper that was being developed. The salesman was of course very interested for his customer and was paying frequent visits to the research department to see what new innovation he could take to his customer.

Well, the research & development department had developed a new formula that would be very good with regard to the chemical properties that were needed. Before continuing, let's take a moment and say how you make money making and selling rubber stoppers. You do it by selling a lot of them! A typical rubber stopper may cost about 3 cents to manufacture, when you manufacture hundreds of thousands of them in a day. Let's say that you are prepared to sell these at 5 cents each. When you receive a continual order for 3 million stoppers per month at 5 cents each on a stopper that cost you 3 cents to make, you can have a nice income. That's from one customer. Remember, you have several customers.

Getting back to our example, the research people were over in the pilot plant getting some stoppers made from this formula, or formulation as it is

Table 15-2. Desirable relationship

Subject	R&D	Marketing	Legal	Sales	Manufacturing	Finance
New Product Design	Let's meet with manufacturing to make sure we design something they can produce.		Let's talk about this design thoroughly before hitting the market with it.	R&D listens to us and I believe we're coming out with a new product soon.		
Business Trips to Customers	We appreciate sales and marketing having us talk to the customer one-on-one.	The research people are a big help in explaining the technicalities to the customers.	We are always cautious but we have confidence in our technical people.			Some of those R&D people really seem to understand that things cost money and they don't always expect to fly first class.
New Production equipment	Good! Manufacturing is going to make the products we invented.	Good! Manufacturing is going to make the products we're marketing.			This will help us maintain full employment and produce quality products.	

Table 15-2. Continued

Subject	R&D	Marketing	Legal	Sales	Manufacturing	Finance
Advertising and Promotion		Working with our R&D people helps us to design our promotional strategy.	We may have to be conservative but we trust our technical and our marketing persons.		Let's sell a lot of product so we can keep the plant running with full employment.	
New Product Testing			We're confident that our product is a safe one.	We have good data that tells both us and our customer about the product.	Things are running smoothly, thanks to the advanced testing.	A worthwhile investment. It will save us money in the long run.

called. The persons in the pilot plant had sorted out the undesirables, or the imperfects, and had produced a box filled a few hundred real good looking stoppers. What had not yet been recorded was *that for every good one produced, nine were imperfect and had to be thrown out!* This represents a 90% reject level. To produce stoppers at 3 cents each cost to the manufacturer but to have only one out of ten be a good one, really means a true cost of 30 cents each. This information had not yet been conveyed from the pilot plant to the research department. The salesman visited the pilot plant and saw the good ones, in fact, took about 100 of them, and ran off the customer. The customer liked the looks of them, and on some accelerated testing on the basis of the 100 "sample" stoppers, placed a very large order.

Now, take a close look at the situation. The salesman had a very large order, 10 million stoppers, for stoppers that he thought would cost 3 cents each that he was selling for 5 cents each, making a nice profit. There were going to be future orders of course. In reality, the salesman had sold a stopper for 5 cents each that cost 30 cents each to make. This presents a problem.

The problem here was rectified by the salesman going to the customer sheepishly and apologetically saying that he had acted prematurely and that the formulation was not yet ready to sell to a customer. However, the customer had almost set up a production schedule of pharmaceutical product in vials using this new stopper. Had that occurred, it would have cost the customer many dollars to change back since some of the handling systems had to be modified for this different formulation. This is an example of the type of problem that can occur and this is a real example that actually did occur.

The moral of the story is to be careful that piecemeal information is not conveyed from research to the sales or marketing departments or the manufacturing department before all the fine points are worked out.

The converse situation occurs at times. This is where a product is ready to go to the market and there is a timidity on the part of some of the company management to go to the market until the product is tested ad infinitum. A good case in point is the story that is told around the turn of the century about the harness maker who determined that he wanted to make the finest harness around. He isolated himself in his workshop for 3 years not venturing out for anything and having his spouse bring his food into him. He had made several harnesses that were of high quality but was determined to have the best around. It took 3 years to do this. At the end of the 3 years when he emerged from his workshop with the finest harness around, he looked out into the streets and was surprised at the sight he beheld. People were not riding horses anymore! This new horseless carriage, which we now call a car, was the conveyance that was being used to transport people and there was no need for his harness.

This does happen today with some products where management does have a good product and is fearful of going to the market too soon and what results is that a competitor—often with a lesser quality product—beats this producer to the market and captures the market share.

What these two examples are saying is that *timeliness* is a key factor along with the proper conveyance of information from one department to another. These interrelationships exist when a company first starts but sometimes diminish as a company grows bigger. Remember the mobile back in Chapter 1 that showed the various disciplines or divisions or departments and it was mentioned that if one part of the mobile is displaced, then the whole mobile must shift in order to regain equilibrium? Well, that's what we are talking about here. An unexpected shift is too big a disruption. But a shift that is planned can be accommodated for by the other divisions or departments.

The best way to avoid any problems is to have communication among the various divisions. More will be said about communication in the next chapter, but for now, suffice it to say that communication among the various functions facilitates getting a new product to the market, or modifying an existing product, and thereby facilitates the company making a lot of money, which after all, is why the company exists.

CHAPTER 16

People Skills: How to Get Along With Others
(The Most Important Chapter in This Book)

GENERAL

It's an established fact that as persons move up the ladder of success they rely more and more on their "people skills," (i.e., the ability to get along with others), than they do on their technical competence. Actually, you can say it another way. As persons rely more and more on their people skills, they move up the ladder of success faster and higher.

A few years ago a graduate school of the University of Michigan asked over 1100 executives which courses they felt prepared a person for business leadership. The most common response with a rating or 71% was Business Communication. The second highest with a rating of 64% was Finance. The former is contained in this chapter and the latter is Chapter 4 of this book.

In his book *Growing a Business,* Simon and Schuster, 1987, Paul Hawken discusses business plans and marketing plans. In the part that contains the discussion on the competitive analysis section of the marketing plan, Paul says, "Ironically, the reader will learn more from this section about the character of the writer than about the character of the competition." Here, the communication between the writer and the reader conveys not just what the writer intends to present to the reader about the marketing plan itself, but communicates to the reader something about the writer.

Doesn't a painting in a museum communicate something about the painter? Don't depressed people paint depressing scenes and happy people paint happy scenes? Don't depressed song writers write sad songs and contented song writers write happy songs? What you produce, whether a painting, or a song, or a poem, or a marketing plan, tells a lot more than your fundamental message. You are communicating something about yourself.

A way of remembering how important people skills are is to remember that the best things in life that ever happen to you are a result of getting someone else to say "yes" to something you propose to them. Conversely, some of the most disappointing times in your life happen when people say "no" to a suggestion of yours. Doesn't it seem logical to learn how to make people give you the answer you want?

Getting along with others covers a lot of territory. You want to get along with others

- at home, in family life
- at work
- at civic functions
- driving on the expressway
- and many other places and situations that will occur to you

In the early 1900s, Andrew Carnegie paid Charles Schwab $1,000,000 a year to manage a steel company. Charles Schwab had a way of getting things done. He readily admitted that it was his ability to deal with people that contributed to his success. In the early 1900s, $1,000,000 a year was a very large salary, even for an executive of a steel company.

You have to have some knowledge, in fact, a reasonable knowledge about your primary field of endeavor. However, the ability to have people do what you want them to do and to like doing that is a talent that will bring much success to you, both in personal satisfaction and professional advancement.

Getting along with others involves, from a management viewpoint, getting others to do what you want them to do and have them liking it. This admittedly is easier in some situations than in others, however, it is always the best way. While in some cases it takes more effort and is not as fully successful as in other cases, it is the best policy.

LISTENING

The next section of this chapter is called communicating, and listening is part of the communications process. However, listening is so important that we are considering it here as a separate topic within this chapter.

It has been said that you have two ears and one mouth and that you should use them proportionately. For calculation purposes this means that of your listening and talking time, two thirds of it should be spent listening to others. This equates to twice as much listening as speaking.

Listening, as we are describing it here not only refers to listening instead of speaking but refers to reading what other people have written before you sit down and write something in return. For brevity here we will use the terms listening and speaking but you know that it also applies to the written word.

Before describing the advantages of listening in more detail, let's take a few typical questions that have been asked of me and you will be provided with the answers to these questions:

Q. When I am in a conversation with someone in a one-to-one talk, I have difficulty in knowing what to do with my hands. What do I do?

A. All you have to do is place one hand somewhere and know that it is there. This can be on the arm of the chair or on your knee or someplace where you know that hand is. The other hand will take care of itself and won't get you in trouble. Most times when you fidget it is when both hands are going at the same time.

Q. Where do I look when I am in a conversation?

A. An easy thing to remember is when you are talking look into the person's eyes. And when he is talking look into his mouth because that is where the sound is coming from. Of course, if he is showing you a form or letter you will look at what he is showing you but in normal conversation do what we have just said and you will find it very easy to speak and listen to someone.

Q. In some cases, with some very high up people I still feel a little uneasy. What do I do?

A. Carry a tablet or a manila folder or a portfolio type folder with you. This not only gives you something to do with your hands, it gives you something to write on if you decide to take notes. It immediately conveys your interest to the other person. Be cautious not to immediately start writing down too many notes. This will detract from your listening and you won't hear everything that is being said.

If you take any notes at all, take only a few. In fact, if you don't take any notes, the tablet will still have served a purpose—it showed your interest and still permitted you to look at the person speaking and listen to that person.

There are times when other persons who are speaking to us have some things about them that can distract us from listening. One of these things is an accent. If someone is speaking to us and that person has a heavy accent, we sometimes will not listen as well as perhaps we should. Has this ever happened to you? Have you ever done that...turned off a person because they had an accent and it was too much trouble for you to listen? As you answer these, think of this—does the fact that they have an accent mean that what they are saying is not important? If you believe that a person, regardless of accent or no accent, does not have anything worth-while listening to, then don't listen to that person in the first place. Why should you waste your time? If however, you believe that the person does have something important to say, then, regardless of accent or no accent, perhaps you should try to listen. When a person with a heavy accent is speaking to you and you have trouble understanding him keep in mind that he knows he has an accent, so, say to him something like, "I am interested in what you have to say but I am having trouble understanding you through your accent. Could you repeat that a little more slowly for me?" You have just told the person that you want to hear him and you believe what he has to say is important. He is not going to walk away in disgust. He is going to speak slowly and more clearly so that you can understand what he has to say. Try it. It works very well.

The same situation as described above works with people who have a speech impediment, with persons that are speaking to you with a noisy production environment in the background, and in a variety of cases where it does require a good effort on your part and some effort on the other person's part for you to listen to what that person has to say. Keep in mind what we discussed above. The person knows that there is a distraction. Just let him know that you want to hear what he has to say and ask him to do whatever you feel is right, to speak more slowly, to speak more clearly, to move away from the background noise, or whatever. He will appreciate you saying this so that he can tell you what he has to say and you will hear and understand him.

There are some keys to effective listening that will develop good listening habits for you. They are listed in Table 16-1. It's pretty much self-explanatory. As you review Table 16-1 and you attempt to assess how

Table 16-1. Ten Keys to Effective Listening[a]

Ten Keys to Effective Listening	The Bad Listener	The Good Listener
1. Find areas of interest	Tunes out dry subjects	Opportunizes: asks "what's in it for me?"
2. Judge content, not delivery	Tunes out if delivery is poor	Judges content, skips over delivery errors
3. Hold your fire	Tends to enter into argument	Doesn't judge until comprehension is complete
4. Listen for ideas	Listens for facts	Listens for central themes
5. Be flexible	Takes intensive notes using only one system	Takes few notes: uses 4 or 5 different systems, depending on speaker
6. Work at listening	Shows no energy output; fakes attention	Works hard; exhibits active body state
7. Resist distractions	Is easily distracted	Fights or avoids distractions; tolerates bad habits; knows how to concentrate
8. Exercise your mind	Resists difficult expository material; seeks light, recreational material	Uses heavier material as exercise for the mind
9. Keep your mind open	Reacts to emotional words	Interprets color words; does not get hung up on them
10. Capitalize on fact. Thought is faster than speech	Tends to daydream with slow speakers	Challenges; anticipates; mentally summarizes; weighs the evidence; listens between the lines to tone of voice

a   These keys are a positive guideline to better listening. In fact they are the heart of developing better listening habits that could last a lifetime.

Table 16-2. How do you rate as a listener?[a] Few Virtues are more prized and less practiced than good listening. This checklist, though certainly not complete, will help you gauge your own listening habits. Try to answer each question objectively.

When taking part in an interview or group conference, do you:

	Usually	Sometimes	Seldom
1. Prepare yourself physically by sitting facing the speaker and making sure you can hear?	☐	☐	☐
2. Watch the speaker as well as listen to him?	☐	☐	☐
3. Decide from the speaker's appearance and delivery whether or not what he has to say is worthwhile?	☐	☐	☐
4. Listen primarily for ideas and underlying feelings?	☐	☐	☐
5. Determine your own bias, if any, and try to allow for it?	☐	☐	☐
6. Keep your mind on what the speaker is saying?	☐	☐	☐
7. Interrupt immediately if you hear a statement you feel is wrong?	☐	☐	☐
8. Make sure before answering that you've taken in the other person's point of view?	☐	☐	☐
9. Try to have the last word?	☐	☐	☐
10. Make a conscious effort to evaluate the logic and credibility of what you hear?	☐	☐	☐

[a] **Scoring your results.** Questions 1, 2, 4, 5, 6, 8, 10—10 points for "usually," 5 for "sometimes," 0 for "seldom." Questions 3, 7, 9—0 points for "usually," 5 for "sometimes," 10 for "seldom." **What your score means.** A score below 70 indicates you have developed some bad listening habits; A score or 70–85 suggests that you listen well but could improve; A score of 90+ means you are an excellent listener.

good you are as a listener, you can refer to Table 16-2 which is a series of questions that you can ask yourself and answer appropriately. It also tells you how to score your answers.

There is an interesting paradox. Most people want to know what is going on in the world around them, yet they are so busy talking that they don't listen, when the art of listening will inform them of what is going on around them. Keep in mind that in your business and technical activities, you make your decisions best by evaluating the information that is available. You find out what information is available by listening.

COMMUNICATIONS

There are five billion people on this planet and sooner or later you are going to have to communicate with some of them.

In this section, we are going to discuss why it would be beneficial for you to communicate effectively. We will look at some examples of communication in your daily work. We will discuss some rules of communication and we will show some examples of communication that could have been erroneous or taken the wrong way if thought was not given before talking. Then, we will look at some ways where you can improve your communication skills if you care to do so.

As you progress through your career, doing good work, in itself, will not project you to stardom. Your abilities must be communicated to the proper persons both within and outside your company. There are at least two reasons why you should communicate effectively:

A—Efficiency in your assigned work

B—Advertising your talents to others; Good PR (Public Relations)

When we say that you should advertise your talents to others, we are not talking about an ego trip. We are talking about doing good work and having the proper people realize that you are doing the good work. In fact, this works in both directions. If you are on your way up the corporate ladder, you want the people higher up to know what talents you have and, by writing good reports, and speaking at conferences (both small and large), you communicate to others the results of your good work. If you are already a President or a Chief Executive Officer, you want to communicate to the people who work for you in your company what your thoughts and directions are. You might say that if you didn't have good communications in the first place you wouldn't be the President or the Chief Executive Officer, but there are some cases when some persons reach these positions in small or newly formed companies and then the company grows and they find that their communication skills are not commensurate with the position that they now hold.

Communications in your daily work can involve:

- Reports
- Memos
- Electronic mail
- Articles for publication
- Talking to others on the phone and in person (don't take this for granted—some persons have trouble with this! Do you know any people like that?)
- Speaking to small groups in a conference room setting
- Presentations to groups of hundreds at large conferences
- Writing books (like this one)

One fundamental point that you must remember in order to be a communicator is that *the responsibility for communicating rests with the person trying to communicate!* For example, to cite what is perhaps an extreme case is to give an example of you being raised in America having English as your native language and you are speaking to a group of persons who speak German and not English. You don't just go up to the podium and say what you want in English, in the belief that if they want to hear you, they will learn English (they probably know English but that is separate from this analysis). If you really want them to understand, then you speak in German or have a translator by your side. Admittedly this is a non-typical case but it does demonstrate the point. Your best bet is to always take the responsibility for communications even when someone else is speaking and you are listening. Listening is an important skill that will be discussed later in this section.

Here are some examples of communication that are listed here for your reading. Did you ever have any communication experiences similar to these?

Example 1

Two people are at a race track. One person says to the other "I know the jockey riding horse number 3 in this race." The other person makes a big bet on horse number 3 which then comes in last. The second person says to the first "I thought you said you knew the jockey?" The first person says "That's right. I do. He's a real nice guy. He can't ride a horse very well, but he sure is a nice guy." In this example, the first person never said the jockey could ride well.

Example 2

Two persons are walking down the street and they see a gentleman in his 40s with white hair, and the conversation goes like this.

First person: "That person looks like President Bill Clinton."
Second person: "That's not Bill Clinton."
First person: "I know that's not Bill Clinton."
Second person: "But you just said it was."
First person: "No, I didn't. I said that person looked like Bill Clinton."
Second person: "I know and I'm telling you it isn't him."
First person: "I never said it was. I said he looked like him."

How many times do you find yourself in something like this when you or someone else says "...looks like..." and it's misinterpreted. Something is assumed. Remember in management and in communications when you break down the word assume it makes an <u>ass</u> out of <u>u</u> and <u>me</u>. You should not only listen to what people *say,* you should be aware of what they *didn't say.*

> *I know that you believe you understand what you think I said,*
> *But I am not sure you realize that what you heard*
> *is not what I meant.*

Example 3

For this example picture three corners of a triangle. This is an equilateral triangle with the sides being 30 miles in length. At one corner is Veterans Stadium, home of the Philadelphia Phillies baseball team and the Philadelphia Eagles football team. At another corner is my home and at another corner is my son Jim's home. I received some tickets to a Philadelphia Eagles football game. It was going to be a real good game so I called Jim and suggested that we meet at the stadium. We agreed that we would meet outside the stadium since I had the tickets in my possession and that we would meet by the 18-feet-high statue of the football player that is outside the stadium. This way we could find each other a half hour before game time even though 65,000 people were entering the stadium to watch the game. Fortunately, before we hung up the phone we each, at the same time, remembered that there are two statues of football players; one a runner and the other a kicker, and they are at opposite ends of the stadium. Now can you picture each of us being there on the proper day at the proper time but at opposite ends of the stadium, outside the stadium, when 65,000 people are filling that stadium for the game. Even after attempting to specify the runner or the kicker, we decided to say the east side of the stadium and we did meet on schedule and enjoyed a very good game.

Example 4

Another case that I saw occur in industry is as follows. The Laboratory was in a building 1 mile from the building where Marketing had its base of operations. The Laboratory Director called the Marketing Director and suggested a meeting. They picked the date and the time which was the following Tuesday at 8:00 a.m. and they agreed to meet..."in the conference room." On Tuesday at 8:00 a.m., each one went to their own conference room in their own building. They waited, and tempers began to flare a little with each division thinking the other division did not care enough to show up on time. Between 8:30 a.m. and 9:00 a.m. they each began to realize that there might have been a communications error, and after making some phone calls, they did decide on which division would stay put and which division would travel to that room and subsequently the meeting commenced (that is began) at shortly after 9:00 a.m. This may seem like a small thing but you have to remember that this is the high priced help that is sitting around non-productively. Much time was wasted and some of the marketing people who had airline flights scheduled for noon almost had to rearrange their flight schedules. A small thing—they simply forgot to mention which conference room!

Example 5

One person believes they are complimenting another by saying "that's a nice tie." The person allegedly receiving the compliment thinks "I really

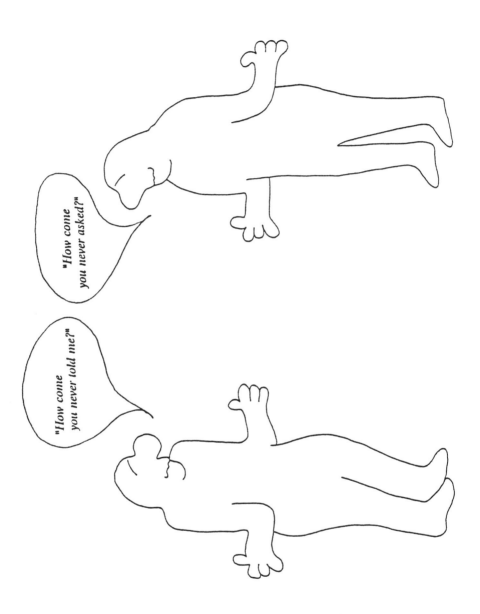

don't like this tie and I am only wearing it because my spouse gave it to me as a present and I don't want any hurt feelings. This person also has poor taste." This is perhaps an extreme case, however, a statement by the first person something like "I like that tie" is non-judgmental and would have been accepted much more readily.

Have you ever confused people without trying to do so? It's easy to confuse people and it is just as easy to simplify what you are trying to say. This happens a lot when a person is not at his desk and you are leaving word with a secretary who:

- May not know you
- Has a little 3″ square pad to write your message on
- Has taken 20 or 30 other messages for the same person for whom you want to leave a message

Many times when we are leaving phone messages for persons, we assume that the person on the other end has absolutely no distractions, when in fact that is not always the case. There can be someone standing next to his desk waiting to speak with him, there can be a computer printer in the background printing out data for something, and there can be another phone ringing in the background. When you are sure you have the person's attention then coolly and calmly state your message, brief and to the point. An example of a message that I recently gave when I had occasion to call the Assistant Dean of the College of Agriculture at Penn State University's main campus in State College, Pennsylvania follows. He and I had previously discussed a delivery system that I had developed for controlling the release of fertilizer around shrubbery. I had forwarded to him, upon his request, more information regarding the system and then he and I would arrange to have the college conduct some testing, the results of which I could use in taking the system to the market. His undergraduate and graduate students would have a good research project and he would have data for a possible journal article. When I called, he was out of town so I left the following message with his secretary who did not know me:

Dr. —
From: Jim Farley
Phone #: —

Reference: (date) phone conversation

Mailed you more detailed information on controlled release fertilizer delivery system.

Patent pending number just received.

When can I visit you to discuss the testing set up?

Do you know any possible licensees?

In this message, I conveyed that the information he requested had been sent and that my patent pending number had been received and I was asking him if he, through his contacts, knew of any companies that might want to be licensees for this product. Think of the phone messages you receive and how many of them seem to come through clear and how many of them are vague to you. Think of how many times the name of the person to whom you are returning a call is incorrect. Now, think of how many times when you are leaving a message for someone else that that message is exactly the way you want it to be. If you are batting 100%, then fine. If not, then just give a little more attention to the thoughts we discussed above.

A few words are in order here about non-verbal communication. Some people rely heavily on body language. That is really to be taken with a grain of salt. Table 16-3 is included here for your reference. The gestures that are listed in Table 16-3 can be taken to indicate the meanings that are given in the same table. Please don't think that they always do. This is given as a general indication. Remember that when these occur that you are in a conversation with the other person and you are looking at their eyes or their mouth and you have a feel for the flow of the conversation. Also keep in mind that that person may be reading your gestures.

There are words that are heard more favorably than other words. Table 16-4 lists words, sweet and sour. See which words you can think of to add to each of these lists. Remember that the true meaning of the word comes out in the context in which it is used. Remember that this chart, like various charts in this book and elsewhere, lists things in their most simplistic form. You will be engaged in conversation (or writing) and you will use these as you see fit.

Well, we have covered here much in the line of verbal communication; written communication parallels that in the sense that you will listen twice as much as you speak and you will read at least twice as much as you write. When to use writing instead of verbal communication is a good thing to know. As a guideline, Table 16-5 is included here. Remember, as with the other tables, it is only a guideline. But, think of it in the situations that you encounter and make your selection appropriately.

Table 16-3. Communication Without Words

Gesture	Meaning
Hand-wringing	Thinking over an idea
Rubbing the nose	Rejection, disagreement
Patting the air	Approval
Steepling of fingers	Feeling of superiority
Rubbing the eyes	An inner desire not to see something that might change one's mind
Fingers interlocked, elbows on the desk	Inward struggle to keep silent
Tugging at shirt cuff	Self-satisfaction
Hitching up trousers	Concern over making a decision
Legs crossed, one foot swinging	Desire to walk away

Table 16-4. Words: Sweet and Sour

Most People Like These Words	Most People Dislike These Words
advantage, appreciate, benefit, capable, confidence, conscientious, cooperation, courtesy, dependable, desirable, ease, economy, effective, efficient, energy, enthusiasm, genuine, helpful, honesty, honor, integrity, justice, kind, loyalty, please, popularity, practical, prestige, progress, reliable, responsible, satisfactory, service, success, superior, useful, valuable, vigor, you, yours	abuse, alibi, allege, apology, beware, blame, cheap, commonplace, complaint, crisis, decline, discredit, dispute, exaggerate, extravagance, failure, fault, fear, fraud, hardship, ignorant, imitation, implicate, impossible, misfortune, negligent, opinionated, prejudiced, retrench, rude, squander, superficial, tardy, timid, unfair, unfortunate, unsuccessful, waste, worry, wrong

Table 16-5. Communication Media

Type	Effectiveness	Examples
1. Written media	Most effective for transmitting lengthy and detailed material	Memoranda, charts, diagrams, bulletins, company newspapers
2. Oral media	Most effective for communications requiring translation and elaboration to be understood by recipients with varying orientation and language skills	Face-to-face discussion, telephone conversations, lectures, conferences
3. Multimedia	Most effective in situations such as settling work disputes, communicating major policy changes, and reprimanding work deficiencies	Written/oral, written/visual, oral/visual, written/oral/visual

When you want to tell people something either verbally or in writing, whether you are telling an individual or a very, very large group of individuals, you simply have to remember three things:

1. What do you want to say?
2. To whom do you want to say it?
3. Do you have their attention?

If you can answer those three questions before speaking or writing, then your effective communications will just about be assured. Certainly, the probability of being understood is far greater than if you didn't give thought to those three questions.

If you choose to try to improve your communications ability here are some suggestions:

1. Be aware. This is perhaps redundant to what was just mentioned above but it is important. Be aware that you have to know what you are saying and that you have to know about the backgrounds of the people to whom you are speaking. A scientist talking to people without a scientific background has to say something vastly differently than would be said to scientific colleagues.

2. Remember when communicating with someone who doesn't have all the information in front of them that they don't see things as clearly as you do.

I do some volunteer work for an organization called Recording for the Blind, RFB, which is a nonprofit organization that helps visually impaired people. These persons subscribe to audio tapes and can learn in that manner from the same books that many of us are blessed to be able to read in a normal fashion. The organization is supported primarily by volunteers who record in a regular recording studio and then the tapes are duplicated for distribution. I remember saying to a person I know who is visually impaired that in describing a bar graph I had to be careful and mention something to the effect of "the blue line is about twice as high as the red line which in turn is twice as high as the green line, etc." She enlightened me when she said, "Jim, that's okay for the people who have at one time been able to see, but what about the people who have never seen, and don't know one color from another?" This was a realization for me. I believe that since that conversation I have improved significantly in my efforts to communicate with visually impaired people. Now I am not trying to tell you where you should direct your volunteer activities, but I am trying to tell you that if you are describing a chart of graph or computer screen to someone on the phone either in a nearby office or across the country and that person doesn't have that chart or information in front of them, you have to describe things in much more detail. Try this some time. Select a page from a book, especially one that has graphs or charts on it and try to describe that to a person who doesn't have that in front of them and is on the other end of your telephone line.

3. Toastmasters International. This is an organization (TM) that has many local groups. Some of them meet one evening a month, some meet two or three evenings a month, some meet at lunch time. The one that I belong to meets from 12 noon to 1:00 p.m. on the second and fourth Wednesdays of every month. Find a local group that meets at such a time that is convenient for you to attend. You can attend as a guest for a few meetings before they will ask you to seriously consider being a member. And being a member only involves a cost of around $15–25 semi-annually. That, in addition to covering administration costs, pays for the monthly toastmasters magazine that is filled with very good articles on speaking and listening.

4. When trying to practice for a presentation, even if it is only a few minute presentation to your peers or to people who work for you, try presenting it to an imaginary person. You will find that vocalizing your thoughts clears them up in your own mind and you will have a clarified idea of what you are going to say. If you have to give a presentation in a conference room or seminar room that you have not been in before, I suggest that you visit that room, the day before or an hour before or whenever, when it's empty, and "get the feel" of the room from the front of the room where you will be making the presentation and at least try your introduction and maybe a minute or so of your presentation. When you give the actual presentation, you will "have been there before" and you will feel much more comfortable and deliver your presentation much more effectively.

5. The 30-second commercial. Whenever you have something to say to someone (again verbal or in writing) or to a group of persons, try condensing your thoughts into 30 seconds and make a 30-second statement on those thoughts. Even if you have a half hour or hour presentation to do, try to be able to tell yourself, or the imaginary person mentioned, or someone you know, what you intend to be talking about and try to do this in 30 seconds. If you can do this, then you know very well what you are going to be talking about and you will have the essence of your presentation clearly in your own mind.

Smart on-the-job communication is not about writing more reports or drafting memos. It's about talking to people to build and sustain a two-way bridge of honest information exchange. The goal is to bring people separated by structural hierarchy together into the same boat sailing toward a common goal.

NEGOTIATING

It has been said that in business you don't get what you deserve, you get what you negotiate.

We said earlier in this chapter that you are communicating all the time. We can say that you are negotiating much of that time. You are negotiating when you want to go to the ball game and your spouse, or whomever, wants to go to the opera. You are negotiating when you have your car on the entrance ramp to the freeway and you are moving along about to enter the lane. Think of how many times during a particular day you are negotiating for something, sometimes with people very close to you and other times with people you don't know.

The object of negotiation is not to have one winner and one loser, nor is it to end up in a situation called compromise. The first thing, win-lose is obvious. The second thing, compromise, involves one or more of the persons "giving up" some things that are important to them and coming away from a discussion dissatisfied to some extent.

Negotiating, on the other hand, results in a win-win situation where both sides feel they have received something they wanted and are both satisfied. There are principles of negotiating, i.e., steps to follow in the negotiation process. We'll go through them here.

Information Gathering

Get as much information as you can about the other side. Find out what they really want. An example of this is when an employer is negotiating with a person to be hired as an executive of the company. The salary is one thing and of course everyone wants more income, but when it gets beyond a point, increasing the salary even more does not have a great effect. Therefore, that is one of the reasons why, in negotiations for a high position such as this we refer to "the package." In some cases, actually, membership in a country club is a good perquisite (perk). Maybe this would cost $5,000 or $6,000 and it would be more effective than a $20,000 increase in the salary offer. You might say that with the $20,000 extra annual income the person could spend $6,000 of it on her own country club membership and still have $14,000 more to spend. However, we said that beyond a point, salary increases do not have the same effect. The country club membership is one thing but the fact that the employer *gave* the membership to the new executive is more important to the executive than the ability to purchase her own membership. So you see, one of the things that this person really wanted was not so much the membership itself, but the fact that the company gave her the membership.

How many times did people think you wanted one thing when you really wanted something else? They didn't ask you and you, for whatever reason, did not tell them exactly what you wanted. Another example occurs in the case of purchasing a home. The seller wants a particular amount for the house. The buyer of the house wants to pay something less than that amount. The negotiations open and sometimes get quite lengthy assuming that the seller needs the money from the sale of the house right away and assuming that the buyer will not offer a penny more than 90% of the asking price; it will be difficult to come to a mutually beneficial situation. However, at times when the situation is discussed and looked into further, it is found that the seller does not need the money immediately and in those cases where the buyer was reluctant to pay the full price because he would have used much of his savings to make the down payment and the resulting monthly payments could be a little bit tight for him, a mutually beneficial situation could be reached. What has been done in cases in the past when these conditions were discovered, was that the transaction could go on with no down payment and the buyer could meet the full price. The monthly payments may be large but the savings that were not drawn upon for the down payment could provide a security cushion for the new buyer. The seller who did not need the money right away received the asking price. This does not happen all the time but it is a case in point where, when each person found out more about the other, an agreement was reached.

Who is the Decision Maker?

If there is more than one person on a side in negotiations, don't assume that the person sitting at the head of the table is the decision maker and don't assume that the people are sharing the decision making responsibilities equally. Sometimes the real decision maker sits on the side of the conference table and lets the assistants do the negotiating but the decision maker has the final say. You have to use your own judgement in cases like this. Sometimes you can get a feel for who the decision maker is because the others will look to that person with eyes that are asking for approval.

At other times, if you don't think that it is proper to come out and say "Are you the primary decision maker?" you might say something to the effect of "If we come to agreement on all the terms in this meeting, are you prepared to sign the contract now?" In this case, they will either say they can, or they should tell you that they have to take it up with higher authority.

Once you find out who the decision maker is, direct all your activities toward that person.

Have Several Issues for Discussion

There is a tendency with many people to want to get to the bottom line fast and to do this by having only one single issue to discuss. Then, to their dismay, they find that they have left themselves no bargaining room. If you want to negotiate successfully, have your central issue "on the table" along with various other issues of lesser significance to you. Always be aware of course, of what your primary issue is, and try to find out what the other person's primary issue is. By doing this you can "give up" some issue or part of your stance on an issue to the other person. This shows that you are willing to give something to that person and, in turn, he will be willing to give some things to you and to modify some of his more rigid positions. This takes time of course but it leads to a successful result.

As an example, if labor is negotiating a new union contract and they want everyone's birthday as a holiday every year, you, as a manager, may initially think that cannot be done. However, think of the trade-off. Maybe you will be willing to give them half-days at times they select. In this case, you have not given a full day but it's a day that they can select. Two things have occurred here. First, you have not given them exactly what they asked for in the sense of a full day and that day being their birthday. The second thing is, however, that you have given them something and that is a half-day that can be selected by them. If they care to select their birthday, they can. The two positive things that have occurred here are that first, the union representative has accomplished something and has not "left the table" about this issue with a resounding "no" for an answer. He has obtained something for his people. The second thing is that you have retained a degree of control by selecting what you have given them and not adhering exactly with what was proposed to you by the other side.

So you see, if you have several issues varying in importance to you and if the other side has several issues varying in importance to them, you can give away or trade off on the smaller issues first. This shows that you are willing to negotiate and want to come about with some settlement, and you will find that it works wonders when you are negotiating.

Always be Prepared to Walk Away

This does not mean that you should get up and walk out of the room in a huff! It does mean that you must always be prepared to coolly and calmly get up from a chair and walk away indicating that everything has not gelled in the negotiations. It is not recommended to do this routinely but there are certain cases where this is appropriate.

Representatives of nations in international negotiations have been known to snap their attaché case closed, excuse themselves from the conference room table, leave the room and the building, and head for the airport. Coolly. Calmly. What they were doing was giving the other persons time to think about this indication of their dissatisfaction. Use this only as a last resort.

A more realistic case is in—let's use real estate again—the purchase of a house. If you are the buyer or potential buyer and you are walking through the house and let your emotions run away and say "Great! Wonderful! Beautiful room!", you have given yourself away and you have left no room to negotiate. If, on the other hand, however excited about this house of your dreams that you may be, you walk calmly and coolly, and the seller (through the agent) is not willing to budge in your favor, then simply indicate that while you have the buying ability and are a person interested in purchasing the property, you are not ready to accept the offer from the seller at this time. You will not prepare an offer of your own. You simply leave the negotiations at the realtor's office or wherever, and say something to the effect of "I am interested, and have the ability to pay, but I see no indication of flexibility on your part or your seller's part so there is no need for further discussion." Unless your demands are way out, you will get an invitation immediately, or later that day, or the next day, to resume negotiations.

Compliment the Other Side After the Negotiations

This is not only a courtesy to the other side; it is planning ahead for the next time you may meet. If you want to see this in action, go to the courthouse and watch some big cases that have just concluded. You may think that one attorney won the case and that the other attorney lost. Outside the courtroom, after the case, they don't treat it that way. They congratulate each other, compliment each other on good presentations, and then go their own way.

This same is true in a National League football game. After the game, the two coaches talk to each other and congratulate each other even though you know that one team won and the other team lost. This is both a courtesy and a planning ahead logical rational action.

Please keep this last item in mind. It is part of the negotiating game.

CONCLUSION

Remember that everyone on this planet is tuned into radio station WIIFM. Actually, what this means is What's In It For Me? This is not a selfish type of thing or a selfish motivation. It is just that everyone looks at something and how it will benefit them. When you find out the WIIFM for the other side and you know your own WIIFM in negotiations and you work toward that, and are willing to give and accept trade-offs, you will have successful negotiations.

CHAPTER 17

...and a Little Bit More

It is hoped that the contents of this book will help you as you go through your career and as you travel through life. Whether you are beginning your career or whether you are entering the initial levels of management or mid-management, whether you are a senior executive or whether you are planning your retirement and trying to determine what you are going to do with your life at this state (I am not nearly at that point yet but I can extrapolate), I hope you will have found the material in this book helpful to you. Now, in this last chapter we present to you what you might call a montage or variety of anecdotes or bits and pieces of wisdom that will hopefully serve in a manner of speaking as the icing on the cake.

Admittedly, there is not in this section, a high degree of order in the presentation of these anecdotes, but they are still very important to you.

You don't always get what you want, but invariably, you will get what you expect!

Ask National Football League coaches or coaches of various sports, both professional or college. They will tell you that everybody *wants* to win. Who's going to tell you they want to lose or they don't care to win? Those that win routinely are those that have prepared themselves properly and actually *expect* to win.

Remember, if you want to avoid disappointments in life, then simply don't expect anything because anything you're ever disappointed about is an expectation that did not come to fruition. Therefore, if you don't expect anything, and   don't plan anything, you should never be disappointed. That's how some people think! That's not you and me! We plan and we practice and rehearse and we expect to accomplish our goals.

The five steps in planning are:

- Where do you want to go?
- What does it take to get there?
- Make the decision.
- Implement (do it).
- Monitor, Feedback.

The characteristics of a professional are tabulated here for your reference:

- Is consistent. This person is very good, and even if not at any given moment the very best, a predictable high performance can always be expected as opposed to others where the performance may exhibit considerable variation from good to not so good.
- Is always prepared.
- Is always on time for the event.
- Uses all available resources. Never wastes anything. For example, the professional does not waste time or energy at excessive numbers of meetings that are nonproductive. The professional attends those meetings which are directly relevant to the goals, and then executes performances leading to the accomplishments of those goals.
- Accepts responsibility; never makes excuses.
- Always concentrates on the goal, i.e., has the ability to focus on what is to be achieved.
- Is organized.
- Is knowledgeable.
- Is objective. Even though this person has personal views on a subject, this person is objective when in the performance of professional duties.
- Is decisive, to include having the courage to make certain decisions in addition to making the decision itself.
- Is self-assured.
- Communicates well, i.e., is articulate.

Are there any that you can add?

Risk. Here's a little something that is presented for your own evaluation:

To laugh is to risk appearing the fool.
To weep is to risk appearing sentimental.
To reach out for another is to risk involvement.

To expose feelings is to risk exposing your true self.
To place your ideas, your dreams before the crowd is to risk loss.
To love is to risk not being loved in return.

To live is to risk dying.
To hope is to risk despair.
To try at all is to risk failure.

But risk we must.

Because the greatest hazard of life is to risk nothing.

Back to Basics. Here's something that I received at a lecture by Ned Frey who has a lecturing and training business and I present it to you for your benefit.

BACK TO BASICS FOR PROFIT IMPROVEMENT

Business is an art as well as a science and a matter or practical experience, judgement, foresight and luck. To be successful in business, we must never forget the basics.

Back to Basics

1. The role of business in a free society is to organize and coordinate the factors of production to produce the goods and services that people want at prices they are willing and able to pay.

2. The wants, needs, and desires of your customers determine and direct business activity. If you satisfy your customers, you will grow and prosper.

Corollary: If your company is <u>not</u> growing and prospering, it is because you are not satisfying your customers in sufficient quantity, for whatever reason.

3. Customers always want the very most for the very least. In this, they are selfish, demanding, ruthless, and disloyal. They will abandon a supplier or vendor whenever they feel they can be served better elsewhere. Customers always make rational decisions, i.e., they are always right. They patronize those individuals and businesses that serve them the best.

Corollary: In a dynamic market, there are always opportunities for those who can find new, better, faster, cheaper ways to serve customers with what they want.

4. As long as there are customer needs unmet or better or cheaper ways to meet them, there are money-making opportunities for you.

5. There are always business opportunities if you are willing to:

A) Lower your demands (prices or wages);
B) Restructure your offerings (new products or services);
C) Change your customers.

6. The purpose of your business is to create customers. Profits are the result of creating enough customers and serving them satisfactorily at prices above total costs of production and distribution.

7. It is not what producers produce but what customers prefer that determine economic activity and economic rewards.

Corollary: Customers pay all wages, not corporations.
Corollary: Everyone has at least one customer.

8. The key to business success has always been: **"Find a Need and Fill It."**

9. Your success will always be determined by:

A) What you do.
B) The demand for your product or service, and

C) The difficulty of replacing you.

10. If you want more profits, you must concentrate on increasing the value of your service. The focus on outward contribution is the hallmark of effective men and women. The Law of Laws is the Law of Compensation, the Law of Sowing and Reaping, the "Iron Law" of human destiny.

11. The market only pays superior rewards for superior goods and services; average rewards for average goods and services. Business success comes from developing excellence in a particular, market related area.

12. Successful people are those who make a habit of doing what failures don't like to do. The master-key to riches is self-discipline, doing what is necessary to achieve your goals.

Attitude. As you move through you career and through life, you will find that where some people look at situations as problems, others look at them as opportunities. Much of what you get out of your career and out of life is THE WAY YOU LOOK AT THINGS! When you first became a manager, you had to look at things differently than when you first started your working career. If you had continued looking at things exactly the same way as when you started your career, you would not have progressed. It was learning how to look at things in this different manner and then subsequently learning again how to look at things as promotions came along that helped you. In fact, adjusting the way you looked at things before the promotion was in a large part responsible for the promotion. Please keep that in mind. It has helped you in the past and it will continue to help you. And if you are saying to yourself that this is simply a description of your attitude you're absolutely correct. It's all about having the proper *attitude.*

Index

227